Off Grid Living

How to Plan and Execute Living Off the Grid

(Learn How to Thrive Living Off the Grid Create a Life of Self Sufficiency and Freedom)

Timothy Cottle

Published By **Oliver Leish**

Timothy Cottle

All Rights Reserved

Off Grid Living: How to Plan and Execute Living Off the Grid (Learn How to Thrive Living Off the Grid Create a Life of Self Sufficiency and Freedom)

ISBN 978-1-998038-28-2

No part of this guidebook shall be reproduced in any form without permission in writing from the publisher except in the case of brief quotations embodied in critical articles or reviews.

Legal & Disclaimer

The information contained in this book is not designed to replace or take the place of any form of medicine or professional medical advice. The information in this book has been provided for educational & entertainment purposes only.

The information contained in this book has been compiled from sources deemed reliable, and it is accurate to the best of the Author's knowledge; however, the Author cannot guarantee its accuracy and validity and cannot be held liable for any errors or omissions. Changes are periodically made to this book. You must consult your doctor or get professional medical advice before using any of the suggested remedies, techniques, or information in this book.

Upon using the information contained in this book, you agree to hold harmless the Author from and against any damages, costs, and expenses, including any legal fees potentially resulting from the application of any of the information provided by this guide. This disclaimer applies to any damages or injury caused by the use and application, whether directly or indirectly, of any advice or information presented, whether for breach of contract, tort, negligence, personal injury, criminal intent, or under any other cause of action.

You agree to accept all risks of using the information presented inside this book. You need to consult a professional medical practitioner in order to ensure you are both able and healthy enough to participate in this program.

Table Of Contents

Chapter 1: Off-The-Grid: What It Consists Of 1

Chapter 2: Pros And Cons Of Living Off-Grid 20

Chapter 3: Finding The Right Location ... 39

Chapter 4: Taking The Bold Step 51

Chapter 5: Living The Off-Grid Life 69

Chapter 6: Every Unique Component You Need To Have A Achievement Off-Grid Lifestyles 91

Chapter 7: Initial Planning 98

Chapter 8: Start Producing Your Own Food 108

Chapter 9: Proven Techniques For Water Supply On Your Homestead 130

Chapter 10: Rainwater Collecting Systems 143

Chapter 11: Generator Maintenance ... 148

Chapter 12: What Is Living Off The Grid? 155

Chapter 13: Pros And Cons Of Living Off The Grid 161

Chapter 14: Moving Out Of The City 171

Chapter 15: Power 177

Chapter 1: Off-The-Grid: What It Consists Of

Escaping social duties and institutions has continuously appealed to some Americans. Historians describe the Plymouth Colony, based totally in 1620, as America's first commune, whose founders left England's restrictive felony hints to set up a desert community on a new continent past the sea. The colony to begin with depended on collectivism and everybody's private duty to hold the territory.

PayPal co-founder Peter Thiel proposed a present day geographical region which include collaborative structures floating in an ocean 2 hundred miles from San Francisco. The network, known as Libertarian Island, may have "loose building codes, no minimum earnings, and only some gun rules."

Thanks to Off-Grid.Net founder and environmentalist Nick Rosen, "residing off the grid" appeared inside the mid-Nineties. From then until now, living off the grid has risen. Practitioners of this off-grid way of life embody cannabis farmers, doomsday preparers, environmentalists, liberals, Maramennonites, and those like us who need to get away the gadget or want a non violent life a protracted way from the metropolis noise. Some off-grid lovers are nomads or loners which can be self-sufficient folks that frequently pass or live in faraway areas. As contributors of a colony or commune, a few have a lower back-to-nature philosophy.

Many human beings outline off-grid as lowering their carbon footprint or the fee of having off the grid. Benjamin Sovacur, founding director of the Vermont Law School's Energy Security and Justice Program, estimates that approximately 3 hundred,000 humans in the U.S. Live off the grid, with 70 to 75 percentage of them due to poverty. Others every live in far flung regions which may be too an extended way to connect with utilities or consciously choose to replace or lessen their use of municipal utilities.

Unless you're inclined to surrender a few or all of the comforts of present day-day lifestyles, which consist of mild, warmth, and instant conversation, unplugging is neither clean nor cheap. While lowering power usage thru the supply of solar panels and windmills is particularly clean, ensuring eating water and casting off human waste are similarly important and similarly complex.

Also, residing off the grid may be illegal, as city fitness and constructing departments require flowing consuming water and approved sanitation techniques. Some human beings were kicked off their abodes for refusing to connect with the grid. According to a have a look at through way of researchers Anthony Vassallo and Rajab Khalilpour, regardless of energy generation era, it might be uneconomical for maximum humans to disconnect from the grid absolutely.

In 2014, According to The U.S. Energy Information Administration, a general U.S. Domestic consumed a mean of 911 kilowatt-hours (kWh) of power monthly at $114.09. According to the Huffington Post, a wind turbine or sun panel able to powering a everyday domestic can fee $25,000 to $30,000 after-tax advantages, no longer such as the fee of batteries which could feature a manner to save energy at the same time as the system isn't running. Consequently, exceptional the maximum devoted and affluent environmentalists are in all likelihood to disconnect from the grid simply.

According to Pika Energy, home proprietor Steve Rowe, who lives in far flung Maine, may additionally need to have desired to live connected to the grid, but it charge an expected $a hundred,000 to get it related. His wind, sun, and battery off-grid structures, designed to duplicate energy availability, fee approximately $seventy five,000 earlier than tax credit rating, or 30 percent of the charge. Rowe moreover said that he became answerable for preserving the tool, which includes putting off snow from the sun panels, oiling the sun trackers, and replacing the water inside the batteries.

Due to developing software program software payments, many house proprietors are looking for strategies to lessen software intake through better insulation, more strength-green merchandise, and new power-keeping conduct. As the prices of sun panels and wind turbines keep to fall, greater house owners are probably to complement their power with renewable energy and reduce their reliance on the national electric powered powered grid without completely disconnecting from it.

Going off the grid and dwelling a easy lifestyles - taking complete obligation for yourself is the pioneering spirit of many. Men and women have left the hustle and bustle of cutting-edge town life looking for the romantic serenity and splendor of pristine nature, on occasion with tragic consequences.

Reasons for off-grid dwelling

Proponents of quitting claim that many blessings accrue to individuals who make a a success transition, some of which encompass:

Smaller ecological footprint: Residents in off-grid generally will be predisposed to live in smaller houses, use a whole lot much less energy, generate a good deal a whole lot much less waste and regularly recycle, however the truth that they use renewable electricity.

Higher non-public pleasure: Being able to navigate and resolve your problems is intellectual empowerment. Working within the international, making topics collectively with your non-public palms, analyzing new competencies like carpentry, canning, and curing meat is comforting and easy. Many are coming across unique creativity and higher popularity.

Reduce strain and anxiety: According to the American Psychological Association, worries about cash and art work are the two most commonplace property of stress in Americans. The economic freedom that consists of residing off the grid and the capability to set up your agenda are big motives you could recall living independently from society. From utility bills to groceries and transportation, the charge of residing is decrease.

Health: People living in the city spend hours sitting at their place of business desks and searching TV night time time after night time, whilst the ones living off-grid can deliver this up in alternate for a greater energetic way of existence. For example, strolling as opposed to the usage of. Also, there can be no such trouble as rapid meals for off-grid residents. As a give up result, these people are an awful lot less likely to make bigger cardiovascular disease, diabetes, osteoporosis, and certain cancers (colon, prostate, and breast).

Requirements for off-grid dwelling

Finding foreign places to stay has multiplied considerably over the past century. Today, those attempting to find to live to tell the story off-grid want to both trespass public or personal land and hazard fines and prison time or acquire sufficient land to stay to inform the tale. Homesteads do no longer exist in the lower 48 states, in spite of the reality that they although do in a lot much less terrific areas like Alaska and northern Canada.

Veterans of Living at the Frontier suggest that an off-grid manner of existence requires:

Accommodation: Depending on the location, inns levels from strong log cabins and reinforced yurts to abandoned minibusses and caravans; while many sleep under the tents, it's far essential to have a habitat to hold you blanketed from threat. Even in case you live within the wasteland, it is vital to apprehend the legal guidelines or pointers which have an impact to your live.

Drinking water: A easy supply of eating water is vital. Before selecting a place, make sure you have got were given got get right of entry to to natural water assets or choose out an area with water transportation. Rainwater harvesting systems are endorsed as many off-grid citizens depend on hand-digging wells; however, you ought to maintain in thoughts that even crystal easy water may have risky micro organism and chemical materials. Therefore it's far vital to boil or deal with your water in advance than ingesting or using it for cooking.

Power (fuel): At the very least, you need a power supply to cook dinner dinner your food and heat your self up as conditions dictate. Some human beings rely totally on herbal assets, on the side of wood or dry animal waste; technological upgrades have made solar energy, wind generators, biodiesel turbines, and micro-hydro structures to be had for off-grid dwelling, albeit at a immoderate price. We can use kerosene in lamps to light up the night time. The choice of energy deliver is based upon on expected usage, rate, and set up requirements.

Food supply: Surviving on simply natural pastime, nuts, berries, and vegetation in those remote places isn't always probable. Relying on herbal food belongings can be tough and threatening. Christopher McCandless lived inside the Alaskan

Veterans of Living at the Frontier suggest that an off-grid manner of existence requires:

Accommodation: Depending on the location, inns levels from strong log cabins and reinforced yurts to abandoned minibusses and caravans; while many sleep under the tents, it's far essential to have a habitat to hold you blanketed from threat. Even in case you live within the wasteland, it is vital to apprehend the legal guidelines or pointers which have an impact to your live.

Drinking water: A easy supply of eating water is vital. Before selecting a place, make sure you have got were given got get right of entry to to natural water assets or choose out an area with water transportation. Rainwater harvesting systems are endorsed as many off-grid citizens depend on hand-digging wells; however, you ought to maintain in thoughts that even crystal easy water may have risky micro organism and chemical materials. Therefore it's far vital to boil or deal with your water in advance than ingesting or using it for cooking.

Power (fuel): At the very least, you need a power supply to cook dinner dinner your food and heat your self up as conditions dictate. Some human beings rely totally on herbal assets, on the side of wood or dry animal waste; technological upgrades have made solar energy, wind generators, biodiesel turbines, and micro-hydro structures to be had for off-grid dwelling, albeit at a immoderate price. We can use kerosene in lamps to light up the night time. The choice of energy deliver is based upon on expected usage, rate, and set up requirements.

Food supply: Surviving on simply natural pastime, nuts, berries, and vegetation in those remote places isn't always probable. Relying on herbal food belongings can be tough and threatening. Christopher McCandless lived inside the Alaskan wilderness, lived on squirrels, porcupines, birds, mushrooms, tree roots, and berries, and died 3 months later after by using way of hazard consuming poisonous wild potato seeds. With food challenges, off-grid professionals advocate beginning a vegetable lawn, growing fruit timber and plants, and analyzing about canning and maintaining meals. Fishing and searching can be an choice at fine times, but it's miles essential to preserve meat whilst such sports sports aren't viable. It is important to have dry food equipped for emergencies.

Garbage disposal: Improper disposal of human waste can result in diseases together with cholera, intestinal worms, leeches, and typhoid. As a cease end result, a long way flung regions can be trouble to numerous waste disposal tips. The maximum not unusual disposal strategies are outdoor lavatories or latrines a long way from residential areas, rivers, streams, and unique water resources. You can burn family waste inside the pit at the identical time as plant waste is modified into compost. Another alternative is to apply a septic tank with a buried leaching website.

Safety: Despite the romance of dwelling in concord with nature, positive ever-present dangers also can befall a clumsy inhabitant. The possible threats variety from wild animals like wolves, bears, cougars, and masses of others., to human outlaws.

Extensive education is critical in case you want a a achievement transition to off-grid life, especially for people or unmarried parents. You have to ensure that you examine survival competencies together with clean carpentry, fishing, searching, gardening, recognizing neighborhood flora, and simple first aid treatment earlier than transferring to a faraway location. It is likewise vital to hold suitable physical circumstance due to the fact residing off-grid often calls with a purpose to undertake strenuous physical art work each day.

It's important to word that residing by myself may be mentally traumatic. Therefore, it isn't always for everyone. Isolation can purpose pressure, anxiety, loneliness, and depression. Participants in the History Channel's "Lonely" series skilled a full style of emotions, with handiest one out of ten people lasting 56 days.

Living anonymously in cutting-edge society is type of impossible till one is inclined to surrender the modern-day conveniences that make life much less complicated and extra secure. These embody home, paintings, car, medical insurance or healthcare, cellular phone, economic institution account, net, and credit score rating playing cards. Children are commonly given a Social Security quantity at starting until their dad and mom are inclined to waive the tax exemption for their care.

Unfortunately, nearly six hundred,000 human beings in the U.S. Live anonymously and stale-the-grid, and it is regularly not through desire. Homeless humans in important cities—many mentally unwell or addicted, are off the grid, napping outdoors, or migrating from community to community in charity shelters. They are usually scavenging for meals in dumpsters and regularly surviving from charitable donations from strangers in cash and groceries.

Some human beings pick out to live off-grid because of the truth, in line with them, "it's far the simplest manner to revel in alive." There are severa memories of people who prevent their technique, sold all their property, and released proper into a "extended-time period tenting enjoy." These humans awaken exterior each day, foraging, wandering the usa on foot, now and again hitching rides or hiding in trains and cars, and staying as social as possible.

If you want to live off-grid and stay off-radar, there are techniques to reduce your traceability without resorting to a few intense measures that exceptional off-grid citizens have taken.

In a worldwide packed with virtual and real-global stalkers, identification theft, and undesirable interest, protecting one's privacy is crucial. So for the sake of privacy, use a moniker.

Using a Moniker: Using a fake name is not illegal, as prolonged as it isn't always to defraud or harm others. For instance, writers and artists frequently use pseudonyms in their paintings, and it's far unlawful to apply a pseudonym on an oath or any jail document. Be wonderful to apply your real name while coping with the government, paying taxes, or receiving exams. Remember to not use your actual call anywhere on the net.

Rent a mailbox: Never display screen your bodily cope with except to pals and own family. Use your passport for authentication as it does no longer consist of your date of shipping or address. If you're to provide facts, do not forget the objectives and whether or not you recollect the request sufficient for confidentiality. In many times, the data you offer to businesses and a few organizations is used for marketing features and may be bought to others for the identical motive.

Avoid using credit cards: Don't write a test, specially your real call and deal with. When viable, use coins for purchases, and if a credit rating score card is wanted, use a pay as you move credit score rating rating card.

Use your phone's privateness settings: Apple and Android telephones have privateness settings that their customers can allow. These days, it is straightforward for hackers to interrupt right right into a cell cellphone or cell community and access private information consisting of phone calls, texts, and pics. Those who're particularly paranoid can rely on "burner" phones, pay as you go phones used for a quick length and then thrown away.

Use a proxy server or VPN on the equal time as having access to the internet: Every pc has a very particular Internet deal with that would song the individual's whereabouts. A proxy server is an intermediary most of the computer and the net, making it tough to find out your place online. Take phrase that A VPN or proxy does now not take away the opportunity. It best reduces the chances of locating someone's area online. You can down load VPN or proxy applications without fee on the net. Experts advise using a paid VPN issuer for max privateness. When you go to social networks, you operate pseudonyms and images. And also, preserve in thoughts in no manner to open emails from people you do now not recognise.

Rely on public transportation: Owning and using a automobile calls for a rustic-issued license and insurance to make it much less tough on the way to music your vicinity and sports activities sports. While generation including automobile-to-vehicle (V2V) and car-to-infrastructure (V2I) communications make riding less tough and more secure, additionally they boom tracking vulnerability. According to IEEE Spectrum, research achieved using off-the-shelf device modified into able to discover the intention automobiles nearly half of of the time, and this generation is enhancing. Therefore, your anonymity and safety are greater guaranteed if you use public transportation than the usage of your automobile.

Going off the grid is more complex than many people count on. Although there are stories of people living independently of public utilities, thriving on my own within the wooded vicinity, or managing to emerge as invisible, the reality may be very particular. Few have the income, capabilities, or readiness to surrender material comforts for a new existence.

There are actual advantages to going off-grid and experiencing nature at its wildest even as retaining privateness regardless of the issues. Reducing our reliance on fossil fuels is vital to our fitness and the survival of our species. Returning to our roots and embracing the coronary heart beat of lifestyles that excites our hearts is nourishing to souls. Keeping our secrets and techniques from the curious public, some of whom will revel in our pain, is vital to our self perception and protection.

Chapter 2: Pros And Cons Of Living Off-Grid

Off-grid dwelling is every appealing and scary, relying on the way you look. Perhaps you want to peer every components to determine if it's miles well clearly worth the problem. Let us preserve in thoughts the blessings and disadvantages of living off the grid.

Benefits of Living Off the Grid

Fight Climate Change

Burning fossil fuels produces greenhouse gasoline emissions that absorb warm temperature from the solar and purpose worldwide temperatures to rise. Recall that 2011 to 2020 have emerge as noted because the warmest on file. And that the planet is now approximately 1.1 degrees Celsius warmer than it become at the cease of the 19th century.

Climate change is already felt global, from severe climate sports activities to sea-degree upward push and biodiversity loss. While weather alternate negatively influences our surroundings, it furthermore affects our health and capacity to broaden food. Additionally, it indirectly influences housing and jobs. Global and man or woman measures are needed to restriction international temperature upward thrust to at least one.Five degrees Celsius.

There is growing attention of the approaching impacts and risks associated with climate alternate, specifically those associated with extreme weather conditions. For this purpose, going off the grid has attracted loads of interest as a way to achieve self-sufficiency and safety from climate activities. For instance, the usage of sun strength and having a battery tool technique you may not lose strength inside the course of a typhoon.

Off-grid dwelling can help fight weather exchange thru lowering carbon footprint and family environmental impact. Off-grid families produce an extended manner less carbon dioxide emissions and associated greenhouse gases than the not unusual metropolis household. Those who pick to stay off-grid are regularly minimalists that stay self sufficient life, including developing their food, elevating their cattle, and recycling and reusing items.

Reduce reliance on fossil fuels

The not unusual U.S. Family produces about 7.5 heaps of carbon dioxide every 12 months. However, off-grid families devour a long way plenty much less power and associated assets than traditional living. When you burst off the grid, you are likely to apply fewer fossil fuels (oil, coal, and herbal gas) for energy that contributes to climate alternate, water, and air pollutants.

This is so because of the fact whilst fossil fuels are even though to be had for cars and domestic system like lawnmowers, they will produce far beneath the quantity generated through the not unusual households the use of the grid.

Reduce greenhouse gasoline emissions

Nearly 20 percentage of U.S. Greenhouse fuel emissions come from residential strength use. Renewable power has end up extra advanced and much less costly, making the transition to off-grid dwelling higher and in addition appealing.

The most famous renewable power supply utilized in off-grid houses is solar electricity. You additionally need battery garage era to harness the solar captured via solar panels. An common home desires at the least batteries to preserve the strength in off-grid dwelling.

While the earlier investment in solar might also additionally seem like plenty, you could recoup your initial funding in solar panels in approximately 3-5 years. Still, investment inside the battery system will take longer to repay.

The benefits of a decentralized easy electricity gadget are many; some of them are reliability, decrease fees, extra autonomy, and reduce emissions. Investing in renewable power permits off-grid citizens to manipulate their power use. Every domestic that installs sun panels reduces the weight on public infrastructure, which reduces name for.

Food

Food structures face hundreds of pressures from non-weather stressors like populace call for to weather exchange pressures. Climate change is already having an impact on food safety around the arena. As the results of weather exchange become apparent, food safety is anticipated to end up an increasingly more vital hassle.

Climate exchange will lessen food production as droughts affect farmers' capability to increase plants and meet production desires. This effects in higher food prices and meals lack of confidence on the same time because the food supply is insufficient to meet call for.

Most humans residing off the grid find food safety as their top priority. It is not unusual for the ones dwelling off-grid to preserve dependable meals assets, which embody produce and livestock.

Some individuals who live off the grid have a hobby farm with chickens, farm animals, and one of a kind farm animals and a vegetable lawn, on the same time as others simplest have one.

Growing your meals will reduce the stress on worldwide deliver chains and notably reduce emissions. For example, while you buy a mango from the grocery keep, bear in mind how a long way a mango has come earlier than you get it.

On the alternative hand, you'll increase end result and greens that wholesome your weather and consume them without traveling. This way cannot produce emissions.

The 4 pillars of meals safety are supply, access, use, and balance. Knowing wherein your meals comes from and the way it's far grown is extremely treasured nowadays, and dwelling off the grid allows you to keep food security with out counting on others.

At the grocery keep, it is not possible to comprehend the awesome of the meals, but while you stay off the grid, you are positive what you've got were given had been given is sparkling, healthful, and of immoderate nice.

Promotes Self-Sufficiency

In contemporary society, it is easy to rely upon public utilities. Everything is to hand and proper away to be had. Most people do not even understand how reliant they're on utilities due to the truth they may be efficiently available.

Living off the grid allows for attaining self-sufficiency due to the reality you are in your very very personal, as you may create resources and generate your strength. So if there may be a power outage or food scarcity at your community grocery save, you may not be affected an awful lot.

Skill improvement

When you stay off the grid, you may have the whole thing at hand as you rely upon your talents. Living off the grid allows you to boom precious, tangible, and sensible skills which consist of B. Canning, gardening, electric powered, mechanical, logging, and foraging/looking. These talents are beneficial due to the reality they growth your self-reliance and assist restriction the impact on the environment.

Live sustainably

A sustainable life-style is an try and lessen an person or society's use of the earth's natural property. Living off-grid is a more sustainable way of life that lets in keep ecosystems and herbal assets for future generations.

It acknowledges our obligation as humans to the surroundings and lets in us emerge as extra environmentally conscious.

Improve mental fitness

Maintaining highbrow fitness is crucial as it assist you to manage strain, have an impact for your bodily health, improve your productiveness, and help you reach your full functionality.

Your environment can impact your nicely-being and highbrow health. For example, metropolis life is frequently related to noise, pollution, crowds, net web page website site visitors, and excessive generation, triggering a few health issues.

Living off-grid can bring loads-needed rhythm and environmental modifications that cease quit end result from a calmer and extra peaceful way of lifestyles that improves highbrow fitness and gives freedom, empowerment, and a feel of purpose that conventional existence doesn't constantly offer.

Going off the grid way doing away with one's home from the hustle and bustle of normal town lifestyles. This way of lifestyles allows you to spend time with nature. Not being related to the grid offers you time to do meaningful art work every day, which permits increase your properly-being.

There is a growing records amongst highbrow health and nutrients. The diets of many Americans encompass processed food that comprise dangerous substances which incorporates sugar, trans fats, preservatives, and additives.

When you increase and consume meals this is easy, organic, and free of chemicals and artificial preservatives, you gain extra from its nutrients. A nutritious weight loss program will gain your physical, highbrow, and emotional health. Spending time tending for your garden may also additionally growth your well-being and connection with nature.

Save coins

Living expenses are growing - from residence costs to power bills, in particular in metropolis areas. Off-grid living will become very low-rate after initial investments in land, housing, and renewable electricity.

Considering that maximum of them produce their energy and broaden their food, the month-to-month charges of living on the grid are minimal.

Practical Living

Off-grid residing is more practical because of the reality you may use sources optimally. Most people residing off the grid observe the 3Rs - lessen, reuse, and recycle, which facilitates keep away from consumerism and decrease useless waste.

Off-grid residing has become an appealing manner of existence for those looking for to reduce their environmental impact and rate of dwelling.

There are not any advantages without dangers. Let's have a have a study a number of the negative elements of off-grid:

Cons/Challenges of dwelling off-grid

Location

Location doesn't examine only to town dwellers. Many suburbs won't allow you to live in a residence with out utilities, so you'll need to find out sufficient rural land to get round the ones prison rules. It is likewise relevant for off-grid human beings to strong the right region for their off-grid life.

Consider how heaps land you want to useful resource your way of life. If you endorse to elevate cattle, you need sufficient land to store their food, offer steady haven, and permit them to graze. You moreover need get right of entry to to a dependable source of water, sufficient region to installation your lawn, and a right way to install a waste manage system.

Energy supply

While you can live off-grid without electricity, strength makes residing off-grid less complicated. Most off-grid oldsters select a sun gadget because of the reality it's far widely regarded as an extended-term funding. However, many alternative electricity alternatives are to be had relying on price range, vicinity, and electricity desires. Check your present day electricity bill to peer how hundreds strength you're the use of and use that as the idea for the kind of electricity configuration you need.

After installing region your strength deliver, you may locate that you're the usage of more power than available. To hold energy, characteristic nice one device at a time and acquire this inside the path of the day to get the maximum out of the sun strength. Use a wooden-burning range for warmth, and attempt fuel in desire to electricity.

Food procurement

Producing your meals is essential at the same time as dwelling off-grid. You can little by little enlarge to supply greater than you want and generate extra income to offset agreement costs with the useful resource of the use of developing a vegetable garden on your house.

One of the maximum crucial traumatic situations you may face at the beginning might be finding enough variety to balance your diet regime. Not all parents can growth cattle within the first few years, but with a cautious plan, you may produce sufficient greens to trade for belongings you cannot offer your self.

Learning to prepare dinner dinner and hold meals from scratch is also an vital potential to make sure you have got sufficient food even as your garden is a exquisite deal less efficient in the route of the off-season.

Water deliver

A reliable water supply nearby is essential. Without water, there can be no plants, no livestock, and, more importantly, now not anything to feed you. Of course, getting ashore with a large supply of clean water may be hard, so maximum off-grid homesteads control to drill wells and use hand pumps to pump water on call for.

Tap water is one of the topics novices leave out the maximum, but if you have a generator, you could get a confined quantity of faucet water so long as you don't mind spending cash on diesel.

A exceptional way to recycle water and make certain you've got were given enough is to installation a greywater gadget that makes use of wastewater out of your kitchen and laundry to water gardens and flush toilets - in case you do no longer use automated composting bathrooms.

The last difficulty to preserve in thoughts is whether or no longer you have the proper to use the water on your land. If your private home has a water deliver, you can generally use it your self.

Time management

The off-grid jobs you do are same to more than one entire-time jobs requiring particular time manage abilities to make sure the entirety runs smoothly. Procrastination has no area in off-grid living; you need to plant seeds on time, animals ought to be fed and milked regularly, shelters and enclosures are needed to maintain predators away, and also you want to preserve harvests at a few stage inside the less heat months.

To discover enough time in the day, you have to be a morning individual. Getting the maximum out of your home calls for steady making plans for months and from time to time years in advance. For making plans purposes, maintain positive records of climate situations, harvests, and livestock beginning prices.

Budget

A a whole lot less complicated existence does no longer usually propose a cheaper existence. A existence off the grid is over-romanticized, so novices ought to not forget about the excessive up-the front investment and ongoing charges of elevating farm animals and developing vegetation.

Setting up the power supply is generally the most crucial charge you'll incur. Depending on the size of your off-grid domestic and your energy desires, you may need 15 to 30 massive sun panels to provide sufficient strength to run your own home. You may also need a generator for backup electricity, that could charge you loads of dollars.

If you can't make a brilliant prematurely investment but desires to break up from town life, you could begin via taking smaller steps of the agricultural life-style. Start growing and cooking meals, reduce your carbon footprint with zero-waste hints, and pay extra interest to electricity use. Taking preparatory steps like this earlier than entire commitment to an off-grid way of lifestyles let you keep on facility payments and adapt to an off-grid mind-set.

Isolation

The final and maximum not noted project you could face is the lack of human interplay. Off-grid dwelling draws thrilling human beings into tight-knit, small corporations. Living off the grid may be a way to interrupt out the hustle and bustle of metropolis lifestyles, but domestic existence is less complicated when you have a fixed of like-minded people sharing the workload.

If you aren't already part of the off-grid network, there are various agencies you may be part of online, and definitely each person interested by dwelling off-grid is welcome. This is a extraordinary manner to find human beings on your vicinity to change products or services which you cannot make yourself. Experienced off-grid experts can also advocate on planting and harvesting and any off-grid prison problems you may have.

Chapter 3: Finding The Right Location

What exactly is a "quality off-grid region"? Is there an area that we are capable of describe as an excellent area? Ideally, a piece of land should have some aspect appealing to make human beings want to stay in it, but you may commonly search for a manner to make it a extraordinary location to construct a cottage.

To find out a really perfect off-grid place, you could are attempting to find the whole United States from east to west. You understand what you need, but occasionally it's miles hard to discover a balance among requirements and luxury and a balance among rate range and location. Like maximum people, you may not manipulate to pay for a huge piece of land. Are you being too choosy about what you need?

Determine your needs. What do you need to get off the grid?

You won't need power-hungry home device like important heating and aircon electronics and all the luxuries of a traditional suburban home. So you have to have a listing of factors to live to inform the story in the barren region.

It's critical to method matters with an open thoughts and note the whole lot realistically. It's not smooth due to the fact it could take longer than you observed to be prepared; it may cost a little a bit extra than you believe you studied, however it want to be better than what you've got available.

A "best off-grid region" isn't one duration suits all. That is, it is all approximately personal preference and balancing what you need with what you need instead of your desires.

Goals can be in particular smooth: to be a hundred% unbiased, spend more time along with your family, and enjoy the tremendous subjects without annoying about loan, bills, and next month's art work.

Like maximum people, at the same time as you crave to be independent, you could want to maintain the social thing of living in a network of humans with comparable desires.

with all of your goals, make sure you prioritize the following:

Water

No animal can stay with out water, and we, as human beings, are not any exception. That's why water is number one in this list. You need community water assets like rivers, streams, lakes, ponds, springs, wells, and plenty of others. Alternatively, you can get a water maker and a big plastic subject to maintain water.

Shelter

Technically, in milder climates, you do no longer even need a safe haven; possibly a windbreak or shelter will suffice to stay on. But in maximum instances, shelters are to guard your on the spot surroundings.

Food

We want to eat to stay on, so you can consider a place wherein wild or nearby plants may be for meals in an emergency. Also, select out a place suitable for growing your food, whether or not or no longer or now not underground or in a greenhouse. I pick out hydroponics systems and it is green, and you can broaden food in nearly any weather with modern-day era.

Recent technology and statistics of conventional constructing and survival techniques allow you to stay nearly anywhere on earth based definitely on your preference. There are even human beings building homes at the water in South America and the relaxation of the arena.

Since you could build pretty loads anywhere in the world, the question is not whether it is possible however what you want and your potential. Some humans like cold weather and snow, a few the warm temperature of the desolate tract, at the same time as others choose the slight tropics.

Once you have diagnosed your desires, you may end up aware about and listing additionally, your "wishes." That is, of direction, very notable from the "needs."

Wants

Equipment and luxuries: on this elegance are strength, heat and bloodless water, massive domestic machine, tv, net, cable, satellite television for computer, snug furniture, and so on.

An expanse of Land: You might also determine to accumulate a big piece of land to be evolved to suit your want. You "do no longer want" hundreds, but you will possibly need one massive sufficient to test with excellent constructing techniques and to extend your ranch if you have one. I accept as proper with it'll help in case you very personal a ranch on your off-grid residence.

Affordability: Anyone can purchase an steeply-priced piece of actual property, but living off-grid way which you do not want a big mortgage each month and are self-enough. You might possibly need an much less pricey property that you could amortize over a few years to interest on essential things like own family.

At this factor, practicality becomes the identifying detail.

Most human beings need a procedure to stay and pay their every day bills, however the goal is to be a hundred% self-sufficient. Hence, the need to have a domestic-based totally business enterprise to maximise the land. Some human beings choose to paintings 9 to 5 until they're capable of help themselves.

If you're experienced or formerly owned a corporation of this nature, it'd help. You want that allows you to make a living at domestic and on your personal to be off the grid. That does not advise you can no longer be contributing to society anyway. Creating products and presenting offerings from your area for the close by monetary gadget is a part of the off-grid way of life.

The Internet

The internet and excessive-give up technology have allowed human beings to reconsider the manner they live as a society and feature produced a excellent cultural shift. It is now viable to stay to inform the tale off the grid, thrive, and live a incredible lifestyles. The net has enabled humans to reach loads of lots and lots of others worldwide, expanding everybody's horizons and imparting possibilities extremely good in human statistics.

Off-grid tech lifestyles

Combining high era with an internet-based totally project method you can live almost anywhere globally. Now that humans can efficaciously do that, I remember it will appreciably make contributions to the general monetary stability of the complete populace, which consist of network and global businesses. This is likewise right if such someone contributes to society with treasured services and products.

Start a Home Based Business

Living off-grid, proudly proudly proudly owning your business organisation, and ensuring self-sufficiency are a part of the American dream and the dream of tens of masses of hundreds. People need their independence, however additionally they want the social elements of life. The internet presents this social connection and permits people to hold their personal lives private.

Our global is smaller now due to era. It permits humans to journey and communicate with the press of a mouse or through dialing a cellular range.

We are unexpectedly becoming a cell society, and a number of us see this as an first rate possibility. Earn a dwelling on the identical time as we cope with and spend time with our circle of relatives.

Energy is crucial, and maximum off-grid facilities will generate their electricity, so pick out a region with top wind or sun capacity. This is the maximum essential element next for your water supply.

So, how do you choose that extremely good off-the-grid place?

If viable, pick out out an area wherein homes are less expensive. If you play it nicely, you might be capable of convey companies and similarly settlers to the region, making the land more treasured.

Choose houses with first rate functionality for wind or solar power because the case may be.

•Choose a region with a mild weather, extremely good winters, or snow, so that you do now not should shovel snow each day to stress spherical your house or into metropolis.

•Choose a relative vicinity toward numerous famous country wide parks and tourist points of interest that provide hundreds of out of doors adventures. If the region becomes a center of enchantment for humans, it finally becomes a deliver of earnings for the off-grid community.

•Choose a place with a lower population density however a close-by developing city and amazing capacity for enlargement.

•Pick an area close to sufficient to a buying distance to resultseasily stock up on weekly substances or if you're on the town for dinner or a movie.

- Choose a place in which the land is lovely. Not too warm in summer time, not too bloodless in iciness, and lots of timber and grass.

Manage your freshwater

Access to easy water is crucial. Depending on in that you stay, presenting your supply of easy water can be hard. However, there are numerous options available.

Freshwater supply

If you are living in a rural region, you probable dug a nicely some time ago. You can draw water from the aquifer and electric powered pumps thru pipes into the wells.

Another choice to fill up the wells is to accumulate and deal with rainwater. Remember, to be off the grid manner you have to have and accumulate your water deliver. Not all locations receives enough rainfall to make this a possible alternative, and in a few locations, the practice may moreover additionally additionally be illegal.

There are masses of truck stops, rest regions, and campgrounds with water if you're cell. That may also advocate filling a portable tank or a mobile unit's tank with water; they may be usually convenient and inexpensive.

Conserve water

Addressing restrained water substances while doing regular the usage of manner finding strategies to preserve the water. The greater water you waste, the extra you need to worry about filling the tank once more. You need hundreds of water for clean matters which includes the dishes and short showers, so it makes sense to have a water conservation approach.

Chapter 4: Taking The Bold Step

Living off the grid requires cautious making plans and schooling. It's now not quite a great deal resigning your self to a cabin in the woods, and you could but revel in civilization whilst unbiased of the community grid. It takes a whole lot of artwork: real self-sufficiency calls for self-control and some preliminary investment. After consulting with a few skilled off-grid dad and mom, I've listed topics to look out for earlier than going without a doubt off-grid.

Buy or build off-grid housing.

Shelter is one of the easy wishes; You need a roof over your head, an area to stay, sleep, prepare and store meals, and further. How have to the living place be?- masses is predicated upon to your fee variety and goals.

Small house

Many humans living off-grid pick to buy or assemble a domestic that doesn't require a ten-yr mortgage. A tiny residence is a small dwelling vicinity, once in a while no larger than a ordinary living room. While residing in a tiny room can be difficult, it is no tougher than living in a trendy "RV." You also can additionally want to take a more minimalist technique on your devices. Living in such an area method you could bypass effortlessly to 3 distinctive u . S . Or town. A supportive and inviting community is a bigger element to be taken into consideration because of the fact you can't sit in a tiny residence 24 hours a day.

Cabin

A cottage is a traditional off-grid domestic, pretty harking back to a tiny residence however typically more secluded. Many proud cottage proprietors bring together their very very personal homes, from time to time using nearby wood. It's a totally particular achievement that makes you experience like a pioneer. While a few human beings use their cabins as summer season tour spots, a true off-grid man or woman can use them one year a 12 months. The populace of many huts hunted, fished, farmed, accrued, and lived at the land. In addition to building cabins, you could strive building your fixtures, kitchens, outbuildings, and different things. It's truely an off-grid revel in!

Container

The field gives a short residing answer; the packing containers do not require cutting down any wooden, so it is more environmentally first-rate than the hut. They are already fashioned like a residence however require little adjustment and can quick rework into a comfortable residing location. You can with out hassle buy them for a lesser charge than a tiny residence; they'll be moved without issue for your off-grid vicinity. And for parents which is probably innovative and need to extend, you can acquire what's going to appear to be a huge building through way of connecting or stacking more than one packing containers together; it can be a notable solution, especially at the same time as there is now not sufficient money.

RV

A entertainment vehicle may be suitable for those who need to stay independently without any limit. You should buy a completely furnished RV and begin the usage of it right away (not like a cottage you need to installation after it is built). The RV may be parked inside the scenic location and activate in the morning. You don't want to pay rent or local taxes, however you need to pay for gas. In other phrases, you could stay inside the RV entire time. A correct cell home includes:

- Living or eating area

- Sleeping place

- Kitchen (with refrigerator and range)
- Toilet
- Shower

Of path, this listing isn't always exhaustive, as you could turn your automobile right into an entire home on wheels with all the luxuries. RVs are steeply-priced, but they are a splendid answer for off-grid living.

It's also important to maintain in thoughts which you do now not need to buy an RV, specifically if you need it as a short dwelling solution. Renting an RV is a much less luxurious and more less expensive alternative. From my private experience, I pretty endorse finding out a few RV income web web sites wherein you can discover an RV that fits your goals and fee variety. A similar but smaller answer is off-grid residing in a van.

Build water deliver

Water is every other survival problem that you need to make sure. You want masses of water for eating, bathing, cooking, and agricultural functions. A simple and less highly-priced answer is to place empty buckets and accumulate rainwater. A more superior answer is to make the roof of your private home stepped or bowl-common to allow for smooth collection.

Digging a well is likewise an exciting choice. You will pay a person to dig a well for you, and it may cost a touch you lots of greenbacks, however it's miles worth it.

Drilling the wells in a few places is greater difficult than in others, so the rate you pay steady with foot of drilled hole varies. Freshwater from the well can meet private and agricultural goals.

An crucial issue to bear in thoughts is to purify your water. It can offer you with smooth water all 12 months round. If you stay close to a herbal water source, it could appear to be you hit the jackpot. If you live with the resource of the sea, hold in mind desalination era - it's far now not as expensive because it modified into.

If you're no longer planning to relocate fast, preserve in thoughts developing perennial wooden round your garden - they'll guide you for years.

You can also increase dozens of delicious and nutrient-dense vegetables. Greens, reds, leafy vegetables, and root veggies, are a healthful type of nutrients and vitamins you could rely on.

If you do no longer need to be 100% vegetarian, you may preserve chickens and livestock. They will provide eggs, meat, milk, and so on as a part of your necessity.

Another advantage of proudly proudly owning your herbal farm is that you can alternate it thru barter with exceptional community members. So you do now not need to develop each possible fruit, vegetable, or animal. Instead, develop some and trade them for merchandise your property could not have or distinct gadgets and services you want. It is an sincere shopping for and promoting device free from economic and authorities oversight.

Also, you could always hunt or fish in the forest. Beware! Research on which mushrooms and berries are appropriate for consuming. Check neighborhood criminal pointers for fishing and searching seasons, and do no longer unnecessarily harm herbal international round you.

Connect to Free Energy

Living off-grid regularly way you gather and generate your energy. The most common technique is the ever-famous sun panel. They do now not cost loads to install, and solar panels have grow to be greater available and cheaper. Solar power is free and smooth, preserving you a hundred% off the grid. On cloudy and wet days, you'll furthermore want batteries or generators.

Alternative electricity is the essence of environmentally friendly off-grid residing. Plus, you may keep an entire lot of cash in the long run. Solar modules have end up much less highly-priced and do now not require common opportunity and protection. You can growth your solar intake thru which includes an increasing number of panels - ensure your contemporary electricity inverter is as tons because the undertaking.

There is a couple of way to harness sun energy. You can seize the sun's rays with a warmth water heating gadget that directs warmth into the tank to provide you with heat water ultimately of the day.

You also can layout your rental to make the first-class use of the sun, called passive solar format. Use home windows, warmth chimneys, and warmth blocks to kick back or warmth your house in an green manner freed from rate.

Wind mills are some other wonderful electricity solution, a turbine big sufficient to strength your entire condo. As stated in advance, the use of a small turbine, you could pump water out of the properly. You can contact your close by turbine provider to explain your desires and get the proper quote.

If you are involved that neither the solar nor the wind might be to be had to you all of the time, you may experience the incredible of every worlds through using installing the ECO LLC 850W Hybrid Solar-Wind Kit (available on Amazon). This great hybrid answer consists of a 400W wind turbine generator and a 150W 18V concentrated sun panel. As an extended way as your power is concerned, regardless of the weather, you're ready. You can outcomes installation this bundle yourself and enjoy loose cleansing power proper away.

Get all of the crucial machine and device.

While it is almost not possible to listing all the gadgets you can want on your new off-grid domestic, right here are a few necessities. Of path, the checklist is based totally upon on how large your own home is and what you plan to do in and spherical it; as an instance, whether or no longer you'll have a personal lawn or now not.

Toolbox

Get a toolbox that nicely organizes all of your essential protection and repair gear. The bundle need to include gear like a Phillips screwdriver, flat head screwdriver, pliers (ideally bladed), crescent wrench, flat wrench, and a hammer of sufficient weight. You additionally need some materials which encompass nails, screws, tape, glue, and so forth. Also, if you may, get a multi-device whose versatility makes it a need to-have survival stuff.

Garden Tools

You will need Shovels, specifically multi-device shovels, selections, hoses, scissors, rakes, gloves, and wheelbarrows. You ought to have at least the above to have a wholesome and clean vegetable patch. You may additionally moreover want a pruning noticed and different comparable equipment when you have wood.

Furniture

Unless you're professional sufficient to build your furnishings, you could want to furnish your new apartment; tables, chairs, and a bed are the minimum requirements to make you feel at home. But sense loose to layout greater to reveal your tiny residence or cottage right right into a suitable home, cabinets, kitchens, curtains, rugs, and additional. Just because of the truth you are off the grid does now not mean you need to exist like a Spartan soldier. Here's an normal off-grid domestic with custom furniture:

Kitchen and pantry

Whether you increase food or purchase it at a nearby marketplace, your house must be stocked with devices to prepare, devour, and preserve food. I'm speakme about fundamental utensils like knives, forks, spoons, plates, and jars. Also, you will need meals education system like spatulas, whisks, tongs, spoons, graters, colanders, and many others. Take a examine your average kitchen. You must embody something you have used more than as speedy as to your list as you prepare for an off-grid domestic.

You must pay precise hobby to the storage of meals. If your lawn produces extra than you could devour proper, your greater meals should now not waste. Foods that do not require refrigeration need to be saved in a dry, cool location, ideally in hermetic boxes or shelves. A small refrigerator powered thru a generator or solar panels may do the trick.

Entertainment and Electronic Devices

It relies upon to your taste. Go along side your favorites to pass the night time time effects. It can be a ebook or perhaps a online game console. Unless you endorse to retire from humanity absolutely, carry your cellular cellphone, which may be vain in some places, despite the fact that. A pc or at least a radio is available in available. Off-grid does not always suggest off current generation.

Also, make certain you've got at least 2 to three advocated survival books and publications. They provide many possibilities to boom your cutting-edge survival expertise and might offer you with a wealth of quantities of information and answers.

Be aware about neighborhood criminal suggestions and policies.

Off-grid is greater than honestly searching for the right tool and growing meals. While it is probably remarkable to stay in a

Whether you increase food or purchase it at a nearby marketplace, your house must be stocked with devices to prepare, devour, and preserve food. I'm speakme about fundamental utensils like knives, forks, spoons, plates, and jars. Also, you will need meals education system like spatulas, whisks, tongs, spoons, graters, colanders, and many others. Take a examine your average kitchen. You must embody something you have used more than as speedy as to your list as you prepare for an off-grid domestic.

You must pay precise hobby to the storage of meals. If your lawn produces extra than you could devour proper, your greater meals should now not waste. Foods that do not require refrigeration need to be saved in a dry, cool location, ideally in hermetic boxes or shelves. A small refrigerator powered thru a generator or solar panels may do the trick.

Entertainment and Electronic Devices

It relies upon to your taste. Go along side your favorites to pass the night time time effects. It can be a ebook or perhaps a online game console. Unless you endorse to retire from humanity absolutely, carry your cellular cellphone, which may be vain in some places, despite the fact that. A pc or at least a radio is available in available. Off-grid does not always suggest off current generation.

Also, make certain you've got at least 2 to three advocated survival books and publications. They provide many possibilities to boom your cutting-edge survival expertise and might offer you with a wealth of quantities of information and answers.

Be aware about neighborhood criminal suggestions and policies.

Off-grid is greater than honestly searching for the right tool and growing meals. While it is probably remarkable to stay in a fantastic global where nobody bothers you, we even though locate ourselves indoors a rustic ruled through folks that make all types of jail pointers.

Therefore, earlier than moving into a cottage, you want to check the legal guidelines and guidelines in every area, county, and u . S .. Your structure have to adhere to 3 constructing codes. Area codes range from parish to parish, so you'll want to make sure your land follows those. It's hard to find out a america free of codes and belongings taxes.

When identifying how plenty to budget for off-grid living, nearby taxes ought to additionally be taken into consideration.

Since it's miles too tough and once in a while illegal to live off the grid in cities, your first-rate wager is to get greater rural belongings. Again, do your studies ahead to discover all of the possible problems and legalities you may face. While it is prison to transport off-grid for your land, it's nevertheless definitely well worth looking at what regulations your network energy board imposes on a residing house like yours. If the close by government is sincerely too restrictive, you could decide to settle somewhere else.

Another element to recollect is whether the neighborhood authority has plans for destiny development in the place and the manner this can have an effect on you. Maybe you take detail in a stretch of unspoiled nature, and then someone is building polluting factories close by, or maybe a modern-day suburb you don't like. Avoid commercial zones; see what kinds of businesses are allowed to installation and make bigger in that particular vicinity.

Speaking of pollutants and industrialization, if you're planning to place your hut or tiny house near a drift — check what's taking location upstream. Are there factories or maybe abandoned mines?

Prepare Yourself Mentally and Physically

The choice to live off-grid is not usually smooth, and it requires a first-rate firmness of thoughts. You are leaving a acquainted surroundings and the comforts and conveniences of modern existence. Maybe you will be a part of an off-grid network or live on my own. Whatever you select, be organized inwardly. There are issues and demanding conditions to triumph over, and I'm no longer absolutely talking about weather and searching.

Being off the grid is a lifestyles-changing revel in. You need to be mentally and emotionally sturdy. You moreover should be bodily equipped and in shape because of the truth you will be doing greater physical work than ever: building, designing, crafting, planting, searching, installing, digging, running - it is an all-day interest that calls for you to be healthy organized, and energized. Ensure to be prepared for any physical or intellectual boundaries you may come upon.

Chapter 5: Living The Off-Grid Life

To stay correctly off-grid, you want to find out a way to feed your self and provide pills and first beneficial aid while crucial. You also find out a manner to cool and warmth yourself to create happiness. It's hard obtainable, but increasingly more human beings are looking for to take risks.

In cutting-edge-day years, we've got have been given seen that inflation can impact the costs of groceries and other devices. We have additionally witnessed meals and gas shortages. That has induced more humans now looking to be self-sufficient, consequently transferring off-grid.

You will rely upon subsistence farming as maximum of your food is produced for your land, with very little outdoor enter or help. They have everything they want and might live for years with out leaving their u . S . Or going to a city. Self-sufficiency requires loads of field and planning. For example, a self-enough domestic need to shop sufficient food for the duration of the warmer months to last wintry weather.

Self-sufficiency and stale-grid dwelling move hand in hand. A self-enough farm generates little waste as possible as waste merchandise are reused. Other requirements like renewable electricity and permaculture are vital to having a properly-functioning off-grid residence.

How many acres of land does a subsistence farm need?

The quantity of land wanted for a subsistence farm depends on who you ask.

The interest and desires you need to your farm may additionally even determine what number of acres you want.

Can you be self-enough on 1 hectare? The answer will depend upon you. If you use each place on an acre and feature some regulations on what you could grow, you may make it artwork.

How many acres of land to grow vegetables?

If you're very green, even 1/4 of an acre is sufficient to boom maximum of the meals for a small circle of relatives.

In a really best international, you could growth enough greens to feed two to 4 human beings in that place.

We say in a great international due to the fact you may now not be capable of use a hundred% of the land, and some of your farms can be shaded with the aid of big timber and covered in wooded vicinity.

Or your floor is probably hilly, swampy, or someplace full of rocks.

How many acres do you need to preserve animals?

You may also want as an entire lot as 50 acres to raise farm animals, specially for large animals like livestock. An character cow goals approximately 4 hectares in keeping with month, and you can see the way it affords up if you have an entire herd.

When considering how a whole lot land is wanted to raise farm animals, do now not just think about the land however in which they may be housed. They additionally want greater pasture to rotate on the same time as grass and weeds develop lower lower lower back within the cleared location. Remember that you could additionally need sufficient land to increase sufficient forage to help your animals live to inform the tale the less heat months.

Other land use

You need to apply the land on your to increase veggies and cattle. Energy is a few different problem to keep in mind. If you operate sun panels, you need to order at least some hundred square meters for them. A small home wishes approximately hundred square feet (18 rectangular meters) of sun panels to be self-sufficient, on the same time as big homes may additionally moreover require 1,000 square feet or more.

Finally, keep in mind the gap you want to live in and shop your property. Your home will likely soak up as a minimum ninety meters (1,000 rectangular feet) of location. There can be several sheds or barns to save all of your gadget and device. You may even need a driveway to enter and go out the belongings.

How to start subsistence farming to your off-grid dwelling

If you dream of having a self-sufficient farm sooner or later, now may be the proper time to make it take place. Even if you presently stay in a city, you can start doing some of those steps.

Get out of debt: in case you want to live a self-enough way of life, you want to pay off your money owed. So you need to put off all credit score rating card and pupil debt in advance than you bypass surely offline. You ought to additionally pay off any vehicle or one in every of a type mortgage you very very personal.

Ideally, you do no longer even need to loan your subsistence farm as you may only be capable of supply in a few thousand bucks a 12 months.

Quit addiction: You should keep away from alcohol and smoking except you need to distill your liquor and grow your tobacco. But it's far excellent to attention first on getting sufficient food to live on.

However, it's not actually tablets and alcohol. You want to moreover limit social media, TV, high-priced coffee from your neighborhood coffee preserve, and associated vices. These topics that are slowly draining your economic organization account aren't wished as you work in your own home.

Get greater exercising: You'll be doing a whole lot of tough bodily difficult art work at the dwelling house; you need to start workout as early as possible in case you are substantially obese or out of form. Otherwise, while your livelihood is based upon on a wholesome body, you may be exhausted and at excessive risk of harm.

Create a Garden: Anyone can do that, even in case you live in a metropolis condominium. You can start developing produces in containers to your balcony; developing your culmination and vegetables is vital to getting the nutrients and minerals you need to your dwelling house. So you can start reading and experimenting early.

Get rid of your lawn: Replace decorative plants with secure to consume flowers; in choice to bushes, plant blueberry and fruit timber which may be suit for human consumption plant life.

Ensure you've got the right capabilities: There's masses to take a look at in case you do now not have an agricultural historical past.

Access to appropriate land and water for self-sufficiency: You have to devise how tons land you need and purchase the right plot.

Ensure a water supply on the assets: A nicely or a river flowing through it is able to be dammed or diverted. You do not want to hazard water shortages throughout droughts or the only 12 months's hotter months.

Buy a good deal less: Self-sufficiency is about being an lousy lot less of a patron and additional of a producer. You may not be capable of deliver many outside assets to your private home. So begin early with a extra minimalist way of lifestyles. Make high quality your circle of relatives is also on board, or they'll be bowled over later.

Fill your own home pond with fish: Once you're off-grid, you may use natural assets like ponds as every other food source; endow the u . S . A . With extra biodiversity.

Raise cows and consume their meat: Meat is expensive, and in case you stay a self-sufficient way of life, you can not want to buy it every week. Determine which meats your family likes the most: chook, pork, beef, turkey, lamb, or some thing. Then calculate how many animals you want to fulfill that want.

Raise your cattle: You don't want to buy new animals each spring. Therefore, it would help to learn how to beautify your farm animals. In this manner, you could have generations of animals on the farm and create a greater sustainable system.

Grow your feed: One of the most essential inputs in raising an animal is feeding. They want land for grazing or animal feed like hay and not unusual grains — possibly both.

Learn to are searching for: Many off-grid places have deer and one in every of a type recreation roaming. This is a further useful resource at the land you need to discover ways to use.

Learn to entice: Catching is like looking, but it'd not require long hours of active sitting and geared up. Trapping is a top notch way to get meat in your own family and a exceptional manner to cope with pests that harm vegetation or livestock.

Learn to butcher your meat: After you decorate or hunt for meat, do no longer take it to the slaughterhouse to manner it for you; you want to discover ways to address and hold all your meat. You have to keep as an entire lot as possible and waste as little as viable.

Produce your recycling facility: Get rid of the idea of off-grid "waste" and begin treating the entirety as a beneficial aid. Unlike within the town, no garbage creditors select out up trash every week; consequently, you want to find out a manner to recycle your waste products.

Learn a way to preserve food: Most of your greens, give up end result, and herbs will ripen in overdue summer time and fall at the equal time. You need to stock up on enough meals on your own family to get thru the wintry climate. Knowing how food is canned, salted, and smoked is important to preventing spoilage.

Gather firewood yourself: If you recommend to use a wooden stove for heating, you need to very personal and manage at the least severa acres of wood. Expect to spend numerous days internal a twelve months decreasing and stacking firewood.

Build sustainable electricity: To be truely self-sufficient, you need to be off the grid, and to be off the grid, you want to be self-enough. That won't continually propose you need to sacrifice the comfort and comfort of electrical electricity; alternatively, you'll want to set up solar panels, windmills, turbines, or unique resources of strength to accumulate and keep it yourself.

Unearth your water: As a minimal, you may want to dig a nicely or two on your home to access groundwater. In addition to digging up your water supply, rainwater harvesting can supplement your water supply, which you could use for watering the flowers and for other features. But relying on in which you stay, you couldn't be capable of stay on twelve months-spherical on rain by myself: you need precise belongings.

Install a composting lavatory: If your private home has a septic tank, it wants to be serviced and drained each three to five months. You can try growing compost bathrooms or particular extra sustainable and self-enough alternatives.

Use permaculture. It is better to artwork with nature in place of in opposition to it to accumulate sustainable development honestly.

Mushroom Growing: Why Mushrooms? Mushrooms are extraordinary protein resources and unique vitamins hard to locate in flowers, and they'll be accurate substitutes for meat in your healthy eating plan. Not many off-grid citizens or farmers to your vicinity are probable to boom them. So they're additionally a precious commodity.

Learn woodworking competencies: While living off the grid, you want to restore many wooden devices, which include barn doorways or fences, once they damage. Also, you'll possibly need to make most of the furniture for your private home.

Cows and goats for cheese: If you want to drink milk or consume cheese, you need animals to make it. Whether you need the milk to be an occasional deal with or a normal part of your weight-reduction plan will decide what number of cows or goats you want.

Beekeeping: Bees produce suit to be eaten honey, and further they produce beeswax, which you can use to make candles, soaps, and distinct products.

Save seeds and broaden antique types: You do not need to depend on a seed agency to broaden your food every year. Make excellent you choose an herbal heirloom seed variety to get commenced.

How are you capable of grow to help yourself? There have to be a few type of staple at the top of your listing. These should be high-carb, immoderate-calorie flowers like wheat, corn, rice, or potatoes. All those seeds have a few thing in commonplace: they may be stored for a long time.

Lettuce and exceptional vegetables offer many vitamins and vitamins which could serve you as you determine to your farm. Therefore, you want the ones high-energy staples for max of your food.

Learn to solve troubles for your very personal: Most human beings residing off the grid learn how to be artisans or jacks of all trades out of necessity. You can't commonly name in a plumber or an electrician. It will fee you masses of cash for every little problem you run into; you could collect a part of this via trial and error.

Make your cleansing cleaning cleaning soap: The materials and strategies used to make the cleansing cleaning soap are smooth.

Cook from scratch: If you are a subsistence farmer, there may not be a meals delivery company. So you will put together nearly all of your private home food at home.

Mend and stitch your garments: You need to change or purchase fabric now and again.

However, reading to restore and stitch your clothes can help amplify the existence of your clothes. There's no motive to throw away multiple jeans virtually due to a tiny hole. You'll be operating inside the dirt and notice not anything but your circle of relatives most of the time. So it's miles okay if your art work garments look a bit tattered.

Foraging: If you've got pretty a few land, opportunities are there might be loads of common healthy to be eaten wild vegetation to be had for harvest. You also can use permaculture to feature extra match to be eaten plants for your landscape.

Drying your garments: Sunlight is a wealthy beneficial useful resource for the farm. You can hang your clothes in the sun to dry. You need to plan your laundry day in step with the weather. In wintry weather, you could air-dry garments interior on a hearth.

Homesteads do now not require an electric dryer.

Think about the way to generate income: Last but no longer least, you may want coins to pay your annual belongings taxes. In some places, you can reduce your agricultural land tax charge by way of the usage of manner of up to 75% in case you meet certain requirements. But there may be a risk that you'll want at least some thousand bucks a three hundred and sixty five days to pay for requirements.

Learn to tan leather: People who preserve cattle don't want to throw away their treasured leather-based-based. You can use them to make gloves, boots, furniture, and so forth.

Make your candles: Candles can be crafted from beeswax, soy wax, and specific herbal waxes that you can make yourself. They are suitable for private use or available on the market to generate profits.

Use maple or birch for syrup: Sugar cane might not be grown to your farm in most climates, and it's also crucial to plot about it.

Cultivation and use of medicinal materials: Like the entirety else, the closest pharmacy is miles away. Therefore, you want to investigate herbal natural remedies. Some plant life are used for the entirety from headaches to reducing blood stress.

Build a root cellar: A cool, dry, and dark vicinity will assist keep food. Things like potatoes, squash, and dried beans keep super in such an surroundings. To no longer be too heat in summer time and now not freeze in wintry weather, you can dig a root cellar.

Learn to trade and negotiate: Whether you are buying and selling vegetables or spending your tough-earned cash, you want to use it as accurately as possible. You must hone your negotiating talents, haggle for what you want at a decrease charge, and convince human beings to pay extra for what you want to promote.

Read often and have a study extra: Living off the grid and being self-enough isn't some thing you may examine as speedy as. You will hold to check and beautify your manner over the years. Be positive to maintain growing and gaining knowledge of to avoid falling into antique conduct.

Take a step lower lower back in time: It is sort of no longer feasible for modern-day machines with complicated electronics to be self-enough. You can't restore circuit forums or damaged LED shows at the farm.

To be really self-sufficient, you want to move once more to washing your clothes by way of hand, the usage of hearth for heat, and plowing your fields with horses or oxen. Some technology like sun panels and batteries can be obligatory in case you need to live in the twenty first century.

However, on every occasion viable, try to use the simplest model of the device with the fewest transferring additives. If they harm, you are much more likely to repair them yourself.

Don't be afraid to invite for help: It's tough to do the whole lot independently with out help but getting assist may want to not need to charge coins. You may be capable of alternate abilties in conjunction with your friends for jobs.

Off-grid heating and cooling

Being cushty off-grid way meeting your heating and cooling desires whilst being as inexperienced as feasible. It can be not smooth, however you may feel happy with cautious making plans.

Before selecting your heating and cooling deliver, step one is to growth the performance of your own home. If you may preserve warmness air within the summer time and bloodless air within the wintry weather, your heating and cooling belongings will art work an lousy lot plenty much less. Tiny houses with higher insulation, new domestic windows, and new doorways are the handiest.

How to create warmth off-grid

There are many strategies to warmth your off-grid home, however few make an remarkable preference. A heater that requires lots of electricity isn't always an fantastic idea due to the fact you generate your electricity. The first rate off-grid heating structures are timber, pellet, propane warmers, biomass stoves, and energetic or passive solar heating structures. Geothermal energy may be the first-class alternative for those searching out renewable energy.

How to stay cool whilst off the grid

Staying cool whilst off the grid manner the usage of enthusiasts and starting domestic domestic home windows. Similar to electric powered space heaters, air conditioners require some of power. If you're a mover, plan to transport somewhere with a milder weather. If you want air conditioning power, consist of it in your tool beforehand of time.

Chapter 6: Every Unique Component You Need To Have A Achievement Off-Grid Lifestyles

While we've got blanketed a few important matters required for off-grid dwelling, there are exceptional topics that we are able to effortlessly overlook however are also pretty vital. These are what we're able to be exploring on this financial ruin.

Ammunition

Many owners have get admission to to firearms in their homes. That need to be the same for you if you live off-grid, especially for the reason that you could must hunt your food. Ammo deliver is usually an incredible aspect due to the fact you by no means realize if ammo or firearms is probably required.

It's generally crucial to stock up in this because of the truth you could use your firearm and distinct ammo in an emergency. Always preserve ammunition in a protection deposit discipline out of the reach of youngsters and strangers.

Baking soda

Another easy-to-stock deliver is baking soda, and this herbal neutralizing powder has many uses if you want to be self-enough or off-grid.

Baking soda can help easy pipes, difficult surfaces, and drains with little water. It moreover has medicinal homes that might relieve heartburn and disinfect raw surrender quit end result and vegetables.

Bleach

Another super stash is bleach. It is used as a natural disinfectant; bleach can help disinfect water and kill germs. Bleach is a cheap proposition right now, however it's miles possibly a heat commodity. The latest pandemic has proven us the importance of bleach in disinfecting and defensive people from sickness. Add bleach bottles for your stash as a essential off-grid item.

Dryer Lint

This is each different stash certainly really worth its golden weight in a survival scenario. Dryer lint which you bought out of your dryer display is an smooth manner to begin a fireplace, and it's far very explosive.

With each few wash cycles, you may accumulate dryer lint for you to function a beneficial igniter. Store the gathered lint in a glass jar or subject to preserve it dry and a long way from flames until you need it for a fireplace.

Duct Tape

Another useful off-grid supply is duct tape. You can use tape to normal cloth or curtains round home home windows and wrap splinted legs or arms after an twist of fate. This deliver is tough to alternative in a survival state of affairs.

It may be with out problem stored, does now not ruin, and is straightforward to feature on your stash. It moreover allows guard or cover holes within the shelter. Duct tape is likewise very useful while repairing ducts or installing region gadgets you may need in an emergency.

Flint

While suits are beneficial in an emergency, rely on a reusable fire deliver instead of a one-time preference. Flint and Steel is a smooth device to keep in your stash, and it'll constantly spark speedy. Keep some of the ones to your stash.

Hydrogen Peroxide

Hydrogen peroxide is an extremely good preference for cleaning wounds or particles in people and livestock. It disinfects wounds that could come to be a primary clinical emergency or infection. This emergency supply is an essential part of your first useful useful resource bundle. Hydrogen peroxide within reason smooth to advantage, and purchasing for huge bottles is a first-rate way to guard your circle of relatives.

Alcohol

Emergency wine garage is beneficial additionally. While alcohol can help calm your nerves, it is also a herbal ache reliever after an twist of fate or infection. It's furthermore a natural disinfectant used on cuts and scrapes to kill bacteria. Alcohol is flammable, and fireplace can be useful while desired, and the spirits do no longer break and are smooth to keep in glass bottles.

Painkillers

Everyone must have right enough first aid and clinical materials at domestic. Painkillers are part of a nicely-stocked first useful useful resource bundle that you could use in an emergency. Make sure you stock up on multiple kinds of ache relievers for adults and kids to ensure anyone in the circle of relatives is protected.

Salt

We all need salt in our diets for proper physical function. Salt is this type of things you possibly won't consider till it's far too overdue. Storing salt is a superb manner to ensure your family's food regimen is wholesome, even off the grid.

Salt with out a brought additives does not expire and is a top notch problem to maintain on the bypass. Salt has many exceptional makes use of, alongside aspect killing poisonous flora, repelling bugs, or maybe putting out oil fires.

Trash Bags

You might probable suppose that rubbish baggage are of little use; you could use them for one-of-a-type capabilities different from their particular layout.

Storing a few boxes of trash bags is an smooth way to prepare for survival. The function of the clutter box liner is to surround topics and preserve them out. Use this accessory as a headscarf to defend yourself from the rain, wrap worn shoes for safety, or drape it over a window as a blackout curtain. Garbage bags can also help preserve the body warmth and guard food from predators in an emergency.

Vinegar

You can use vinegar to clean up litter and disinfect germs. As a herbal purifier, vinegar's acidity makes it very useful. It moreover lets in maintain meals like end result and greens for later use. It's right to inventory up on various vinegar, such as cider and white wine.

All of these are vital components for any emergency, and they assist keep your circle of relatives secure.

Chapter 7: Initial Planning

Priorities come first. Plan in advance, please. Living off the grid is difficult if you do not know how lots coins you've got or wherein you may be staying. Your sources and options may also have an effect at the way you get this living vicinity.

Here are a few hints to useful useful resource with transition planning:

• Organize Your Finances

I consider monetary monetary savings after I recall dwelling off the grid. But as speedy as I started out estimating the fee of some of the favored tool, I observed that it is able to be pretty steeply-priced.

You can start off-grid with maximum of what you need for among $75,000 and $a hundred twenty,000. The size of the assets you're converting and what sort of of the conversion and installation you may carry out yourself will each have an impact at the very last cost.

You will need to make an entire lot of steeply-priced changes so that it will well glide your property off the grid and lead a self-sufficient life. It will possibly take quite some time and cash to transform your gift grid-dependent residence to freestanding strength systems. As a end result, you can need to remember dividing the conversion into levels and operating on every segment one after the other over a period of years.

You will need the important facts, abilties, and machine to do each of those jobs. Hiring a expert to do the paintings is the wonderful method to perform this. Learning the potential and doing the mission your self is an opportunity.

The First Steps to Going Off the Grid Are:

- Power Source

A thorough assessment of your energy use is step one in switching to an impartial power deliver. You can forecast the destiny if you are aware about your present use.

Many off-gridders take some time to apply lots a great deal less strength once they transfer systems.

Buying low-power variations of your gift electric tool or growing era to help you eat a whole lot much less power are alternatives right right here.

You may additionally begin constructing your deliver after what electrics your new deliver will want to guide. Adding a generator in your device will provide you with a backup inside the event of an emergency or a prolonged duration of low mild stages.

- Power Retention

Whatever energy supply you select out out, you'll want a mechanism to keep it. This is particularly actual for sun or wind energy systems. Because the climate is unpredictable, you must have the potential to utilize all the sunshine or wind you may on sooner or later to generate sufficient electricity for use on calm, cloudy days. As a, you could want a number of batteries or a large backup machine unit.

When you've got used all of the energy your private home requires, you could reroute the contemporary to rate the batteries. The extra energy will hold to price your batteries until they're whole.

If, at any time, your property calls for extra power than your panels are producing, which incorporates on a cloudy day, the batteries will fulfill your property's electricity dreams.

The shape of batteries you need is decided by way of:

The amount of energy you make use of on a each day foundation. If you without a doubt need to strength your home for a few hours right here and there, you may not need as many cells as in case you plan to use them for each week or more in some unspecified time in the future of the wintry climate.

- Water Supply

You need to preferably have a spring or properly on your private home to provide crystal easy water. However, in case you are changing an gift house, you could most probable now not have this privilege. Catching and storing rainwater is a common technique to create a self-enough water deliver. If you depend upon rainwater, you ought to keep your water utility associated as a backup in case of an emergency.

If you plan on the usage of rain as a water supply, you've got to plan a way of gathering and storing nearly each drop that falls on any a part of your land. This would likely embody big open water butts, buckets, bins, and guttering.

After collecting the water, you may pick to store it in a large garage tank that could in the end feed your house. A water filtering gadget is required earlier than the use of the water to make sure that it's miles smooth and safe. Some people collect wastewater (gray water) to be filtered, wiped clean, and reused for a secondary use in case you need to make the most of every drop.

- Food

Many people cope with this trouble at the final minute, but the sooner you located it up, the higher. The quicker your farm begins to provide food, the earlier you can begin maintaining and storing it for the destiny. It's proper to complement any of your homegrown deliver with maintain gadgets for so long as you need it, however the earlier you begin your land generating, the less time you may need to attend.

Preparing your garden to present as a whole lot as feasible takes time, strive, and a nicely-idea-out approach. To make production as inexperienced as feasible, you may need to restructure landscape portions. You'll want plant life/seeds, gardening gadget, fertilizer, and a water supply to get began. You might also assemble your compost and water deliver in your land in case you set up a properly balanced gadget, at the side of the ones taught in permaculture or wooded vicinity garden systems.

Housing, equipment, food, and care is probably required for any animals or hen. Chickens are famous on off-grid homesteads due to the truth they are easy to elevate, less expensive, and may offer every eggs and meat.

- Toilets And Sewage Systems

Many residence proprietors disconnect from the grid but keep their sewage connection. This is because of the truth mains sewerage is accessible, and putting in an opportunity may be hard and steeply-priced. If you pick to head off-grid alongside aspect your sewerage, one of the maximum commonplace techniques of managing wastewater is to put in a septic tank.

A septic tank is a massive submerged discipline that collects waste, separates it from any solids, and discharges it into the soil. Some off-gridders make use of compost toilets to address black water waste, followed thru a tool to accumulate and reuse any gray water from showers and sinks, amongst exclusive matters.

Here are a few hints that will help you plan your transition:

- Increase your profits.

- Come up with a budget.

- Cut down on useless residing charges (new clothes, cable TV, ingesting out, and masses of others.)

- Put some cash apart.

- Pay off your debts.

- Investigate off-grid residing (cell domestic, prefab home, low price lands, and lots of others).

- Look into neighborhood guidelines concerning off-grid residing.

- Determine how a long way you want to move off the grid (power, water, sewage, and many others.)

- Determine how far away you desire to live.

- Consider your fitness and the way it'll have an impact in your off-grid way of existence.

- Determine WHY you want to transport off the grid.

- Consider your present day competencies (carpentry, gardening, first beneficial useful resource, and lots of others.).

- Think approximately methods to earn money while residing off-grid.

Chapter 8: Start Producing Your Own Food

Off-grid dwelling normally does no longer need a huge quantity of land. You make do with what you have got. Some can also even argue that dwelling off the grid is our herbal u . S . A .. It is feasible to perform it proper now, the usage of your data of off-grid farming.

Before embarking on an off-grid way of life, you need to first learn how to boom your non-public meals. You can not definitely plant a tomato seed and count on to experience tomatoes for months. That seed need true soil with superb drainage, a steady water deliver, and a few mild loving care. This ebook will move over what makes up an exquisite soil, a way to build up terrific soil with little weeds, how to irrigate your plants, a manner to supply fruits and greens, grains and herbs, the manner to shop and keep food, and animal husbandry.

At the notion, you could have a primary step-via-step plan for even as, how, or maybe wherein to begin residing off the grid.

Testing the Health of the Soil

Before you begin your off-grid farming, you need to first decide the sort of soil you've got. Your plant life will undergo needless pressure if the soil isn't always suitable sufficient. What you need to plant will decide what shape of soil you want. If you scoop up a few dirt and it paperwork a sticky, bendy ball, you've got were given clay soil, which might be very tough to deal with. It drains slowly and compacts quick, necessitating large aeration.

You have sandy soil if it feels and appears grainy and crumbly. It may be very permeable and aerates properly, however it will likely be dry, infertile, and will drain water. If your soil is fluffy and office work a loose ball, it's far loam, that's made from same elements sand, silt, and clay. This soil is right because it maintains water and nutrients while though imparting sufficient drainage and aeration. Sandy loam is right for producing veggies.

Scoop round inches of earth proper into a mason jar to discover the form of soil you've got. Fill the ultimate place in the jar with water. Add a teaspoon of dish detergent to help separate the dust particles. Shake the jar and set it aside for an afternoon. The dirt will cut up, and relying on how thick the various layers are, you may be able to have a have a observe the triumphing qualities of your soil.

Knowing the character of your soil will assist you end up aware about whether or not or now not any modifications are required to achieve the most suitable crop manufacturing. Nevertheless, there are some basically powerful agricultural methods that you need to put into impact into your manner of existence no matter the type of soil you've got were given from the start. Living off the grid is a lot of hard paintings, so that you need to be careful approximately the way you appoint it gradual and energy, allow's mom nature be just proper for you with the useful useful resource of partnering on the aspect of her.

Applying Compost and No-Till Gardening

Your ability to live off the grid will rely on how your garden is installation. You cause to preserve and refill all that the earth gives for you. No-until gardening is the technique of permitting decaying natural remember on the ground generate the maximum updated topsoil layer. Then you quick plant into this residue. You aren't traumatic the worms and bacteria, who're busily running, with the useful resource of no longer tilling the soil.

Any latent weed seeds which is probably firmly buried will keep to stay deeply buried. The longer you adopt a no-until gardening method, the more green your garden can be in coping with weeds, however the truth that the first couple of years may additionally additionally see quite a few weeds. This is as a result of the truth that as plant particles decomposes, it provides some different layer of earth to the weed seeds which are constantly being driven down in the soil. In a experience, composting takes location while the herbal waste is permitted to keep to settle.

You may want to take it a step in addition. Eggshells, food scraps, and diverse things may additionally all be located right away to a compost pile. You have to test your carbon to nitrogen ratios as they decide how rapid your compost decomposes and whether or now not or not it will rot or dry out. For composting and rancid-grid dwelling, animal feces is a splendid and vital fabric.

Irrigation For Plants Is Provided

Watering vegetation all day is the final detail you need to do, even though they want it. You may additionally moreover both take the greater realistic opportunity and installation irrigation drip-tape or overhead irrigation, or you could appoint gravity to go with the flow water from a close-by circulate. It is normally endorsed to art work with the slope of the terrain in region of trying to create a pump, that may be a possibly disaster although it's miles a opportunity. Understanding a manner to expand your very own food includes foreseeing problems and hurdles and finding solutions before they emerge.

Choosing the Crops

Planning your fruit and vegetable gardens can also start on the same time as you are aware of the dominion of your soil and feature embraced wholesome farming practices inclusive of no-till farming.

What is the first step? Look first to locate what flourishes for your place. You can also moreover moreover find out by way of the use of the use of interviewing special close by farmers or via manner of analyzing historic reviews to understand what end up normally farmed there in previous times. Next, determine what you revel in consuming.

You must nurture the meals you enjoy eating even as you first start out. Otherwise, you could lose motivation. How terrible would not it no longer be in case you spent a complete developing season generating completely Swiss chard and beets, but you loathe them masses which you become shopping for kale at the shop?

You want to start experimenting even as you've got gotten the dangle of it and your taste receptors have privy to the easy food you're making equipped. Rotate your plant life to add new elements.

This now not simplest benefits your health however additionally keeps the soil's balance. Alternatively, you could normally feed it on your animals or sell it available on the market.

Herbs

Herbs are vital as they may flavor your everyday recipes to supply a completely amazing delicacies. They also are exceptional, smooth to supply, and wholesome. Having a separate herb lawn is a high-quality idea. Making a herb spiral is a technique for becoming a whole lot of special styles of herbs right into a compact area. The herb spiral is basically a mound of dirt with downward-spiraling stones that make a tiny spiral ramp. This association generates some of environments:

• Dry surrounds (at the top, the water drains all of the manner right right down to the ground) (at the top, the water drains all of the manner all the way right down to the ground).

- A moist place (at the bottom).
- A sunny place.
- A shaded area.

A well placed herb spiral want to be simply outdoor your kitchen just so you'll be tempted to capture a few earlier than beginning a meal. Create a mound of soil that is six toes in diameter and 3 ft immoderate to make a herb spiral. Rocks need to then be positioned in a spiral from pinnacle to bottom. Before planting some component, allow the herb spiral accept a bit at the same time as to avoid soil erosion or settling from absorbing your herb seeds.

In order to influence you to choose up some herbs earlier than making equipped a supper, herb spirals need to be placed strategically proper outside your kitchen. Create a mound of soil this is six ft in diameter and three toes immoderate to make a herb spiral. Rocks must then be placed in a spiral from pinnacle to backside. Before you plant something inside the herb spiral, permit it get hold of a piece length to avoid soil settling or erosion from soaking up your herb seeds.

Veggies and Fruits

Fruit and nut wood should be one of the first items you plant as they might take years to provide fruit. Plan in which your wooden can be positioned in order that they will provide a whole lot of coloration.

Setting up a berry patch is a high-quality concept. Berries are perennial plant life, as a cease result they broaden twelve months after three hundred and sixty five days. They are extraordinary even as dried, frozen, turned into jams, jellies, and preserves, and can be served on their very personal or in pies. If you glide crazy, you may even collect a you-pick out out garden, which can produce extra income that might be useful.

Based on the vitamins that vegetation require to live, veggies can be categorised into numerous groups. To avoid soil depletion, you need to rotate among organizations of heavy feeders, light feeders, and heavy donors.

Crops encompass asparagus, beet, broccoli, maize, strawberries, and okra are amongst your heavy feeders.

Light feeders need to test after the larger feeders:

- Swiss chard; carrots; garlic; leeks; candy potatoes;

Your heavy provider should come after your slight feeders: Alfalfa, beans, clover, peas, peanuts, and beans.

Your heavy vendors are often cowl plants. Cover flowers are vegetation that develop at the ground to reduce soil erosion and compaction even as concurrently replenishing the soil's depleted vitamins, specially at a few degree in the wintry weather months. For farm animals, cowl vegetation may be cultivated and gathered.

- Grains.

When it involves farming grains, there are various myths that want to be debunked. They are extremely clean to expand, to start. Second, you do not need numerous acres. Third, you do no longer want any expensive machine.

Once you have your grain seeds, plant them 6 inches into the dust in a place with loads of mild. Use a seeder (which may resemble a mason jar with holes pierced in the lid) to make sure honest dispersal. When a crop is prepared to be harvested, lessen it with pruning shears or a hedge trimmer (or a few factor similar) (or some component similar).

Next, beat the stalks with a stick to launch the seeds from the plant. Finally, you could dispose of the grain's paper coating with the aid of moving it from one dish to another at the same time as it's miles being blown by using manner of a blower. One bushel of wheat, or more or a lot less 60 kilos of grain, may be produced on one thousand ft of land. With that, I need to make spherical 34 loaves of bread.

Saving Seeds and Storing Crops

Crop storage and seed protection are two of the most essential additives of off-grid survival. You likely won't be capable of consume all of your tomatoes over the summer season, and it's miles implausible that you may be capable of produce more tomatoes within the iciness. Therefore, you may dry tomatoes into chips and use them in salsas and sauces.

You now have tomato paste and sauce for cooking soups and pasta dinners at the identical time as winter hits. Your dried tomatoes may be utilized in hummus dishes, salads, and sandwiches. There are severa techniques to hold vegetation, but we will absolutely pass over a few, collectively with most tremendous storage conditions.

Typically, an airtight container in a cold, dark vicinity is the advanced storage environment. If you do now not have a wine cellar, it's miles traditional, simply make certain to hold them faraway from the oven and domestic domestic windows. A wine cellar is probably incredible. A pantry would in all likelihood suffice truly as well. Be cautious so far and label any preserved objects.

Canning

The boiling pot approach and the strain approach are the two methods for canning. The boiling pot is a consistent manner to maintain tomatoes, stop end result, jams, jellies, pickles, and one-of-a-type preserves; but, strain canning is the handiest technique this is constant to apply for keeping veggies, meats, fowl, and seafood.

To efficiently can all your food, you must comply to specific necessities. Your food will decay or may additionally want to make you extraordinarily sick in case you do not closely follow to those instructions (in all likelihood kill you) (probable kill you). When performed properly, they're a extraordinarily attractive and dependable technique to keep meals for months (and in all likelihood years) to go lower back. They are also quite sincere to have a examine.

Freezing

Almost a few trouble can be frozen, which embody culmination, vegetables, meat, seafood, and herbs. When it involves freezing vegetables first of all, there are some advocated measures to comply with. You can also moreover choose to peel or blanch the vegetable before freezing, relying on the kind.

Fermenting

Another manner of meals protection is fermentation. It is easy to break up a number of veggies, season them with a touch salt and pepper, and throw them in a crock for fermentation. You can have clean sauerkraut or kimchi some weeks later.

Then, the use of one of the aforementioned canning strategies, you can maintain this. Again, there are specific recipes you may make use of to deliver top notch fermented food. They additionally embody a whole lot of probiotics, which makes them fairly beneficial for you.

Drying

Food may be stored properly by way of the use of drying. Although you may dry inside the solar, a meals dehydrator is useful. You can also dry some of substances, together with fruit think fruit leather-primarily based. Beets, sweet potatoes, meat, herbs, and potatoes. A recipe e-book that outlines the proper temperature and drying time is supplied with many meals dehydrators.

In order to keep away from depending simply on canned green beans, it's far important to lease a variety of various protection methods. Although sweet potato and beet chips are simply as tasty as inexperienced beans in a can.

Saving Seeds

Washing and drying seeds earlier than storing them in a sealed, categorized discipline in a fab, dark region is the top notch method to preserve them. Some seeds need to stratify earlier than being transplanted, wherein case freezing is an opportunity. If you adopt the concern of saving your seeds, you can not most effective store coins but furthermore end up absolutely self-reliant.

How Raising Life Stock Can Help You Live Off Grid

If you're new to living off the grid, this can appear like a difficult assignment. Fortunately, if given the possibility, animals can deal with themselves quite darn well. In reality, in case you let them, they may come to be looking after both you and your garden (am simply kidding).

The following animals:

- cows.

- Goats, sheep, pigs, horses, ducks, chickens, goats, and turkeys.

While proudly proudly proudly owning maximum of these livestock can also appear attractive, it's miles first-rate to begin small and with animals that you experience ingesting (yeah, that might sound shape of creepy). Living off the grid has severa advantages, taken into consideration one in each of it is community. Human socialization is important for us as social creatures.

Find out what other farmers to your area are growing. If there are more than one cow farmers inside the region, don't forget about growing pigs, lambs, and turkeys. You may additionally moreover then artwork together to have extra meat after that.

It is critical to carry out a bit in-depth studies on the personalities and wishes of various animals. For example, goats will devour a few thing they come across. Sheep, but, do now not devour the whole thing in sight and additionally provide superb milk for cheese. Not to say, there are various breeds available, some of which Produce greater wool, milk, and meat.

Chickens require particularly little safety. They are ready once they have a coop and some land. They will offer you one egg in step with day and pride to wander freely. They require get entry to to clean water, a honest deliver of calcium and protein, protection from the climate (which encompass colour), and a place to take a dust bathtub. Incredible agricultural fertilizer constituted of chook poo.

Even higher, you could create a chicken tractor, a movable cage that allows the chickens to forage exactly in which you want them to. They urinate at the floor, devour grass and bugs. As brief as you cast off them out of the way, you've got got the proper vicinity for developing flowers: no insects, splendid fertilizer, and almost no grass.

Food Growth for Livestock

It is a wonderful idea to research how you can appoint your private land to feed your cattle. Just like people, animals require a few particular nutrients to flourish and stay healthy. Growing wintry weather cowl vegetation like rye, wheat, and oats is a honest approach to provide a regular deliver of animal feed.

Many dad and mom cultivate extra veggies especially for their farm animals. When it comes time to butcher an animal, you could be confident that it has eaten pretty a few cease end result and veggies instead of grains, preservatives, and chemical substances. Pigs will eat canned meals, on the same time as hens opt for easy veggies and insects.

Save the grass cuttings of your out of doors when you have goats.

Calculating the Workload

Don't permit the expected workload discourage you. The first few years can be traumatic, difficult, and complete of mistakes and disasters. Though the work is seasonal, you may nevertheless installed loads of attempt. It can be busier in the spring and summer season than within the fall and iciness. Your weeks of harvest and meals maintenance may be busier than your weeks of maintenance. There may be severa planning and bodily tough paintings worried, however in case you make use of your animals, observe, communicate with others, accept as genuine with, and ask for resource, the benefits will substantially surpass the strive. You can excellent harvest what you have planted.

Chapter 9: Proven Techniques For Water Supply On Your Homestead

Having an sufficient supply of clean, ingesting water is important whilst living off the grid. Turning on a tap is all it takes for folks who stay off the grid to satiate their thirst or take a easy bathe. However, acquiring and the usage of water will become a pretty greater concerned method if you're deliberating sporting out an off-grid existence.

Where to water Off-Grid:

Unknown to many, there are distinctive off-the-grid water sources. Although wells are the maximum apparent solution, there are pretty a few extra sustainable water supply solutions.

- Well Water

Off-grid water is sort of usually obtained from wells. Since the start of civilization, human beings have used nicely water, and for correct reason. Freshwater is continuously provided from artesian wells.

Wells' number one drawback is the expenses worried. The correct information is that, at the same time as you've constructed via with one, your properly gives water with very little care required. The intensity of your nicely to your area is managed by way of manner of the usage of the nearby water table. The water desk may be as shallow as one hundred feet beneath the ground in wetter places. You may additionally moreover want to drop up to 1,000 feet in places with wilderness situations and unique arid environment.

You need a pump to drag water from your nicely. One of the pinnacle five water pumps to be had on the market is a manual water pump, or you may pick one of the splendid sun-powered or traditional electric water pumps. The seismic and drilling hobby nearby is one remaining trouble to remember about. Your well shaft can be damaged via a large earthquake or with the aid of operations like hydraulic fracturing. When identifying whether or not or no longer a well is proper for you, examine the expenditure instead of the lifespan benefits.

Springs

An herbal spring is amongst the biggest providers of water. A smooth analogy for springs is natural wells. They are regions wherein subsurface water entails the floor through cracks and fractures within the Earth. Depending on their length, springs can also furthermore offer a large quantity of water at no fee to you. With some pipelines and a mechanism to direct the water into garage, it is easy to get this water.

Here's A Quick Description of the Essential Steps:

The biggest Set lower again of natural springs is their scarcity. The bulk of off-grid land parcels will no longer have a spring flowing thru them. Those who do will pay substantially extra than their friends. Springs are also impacted through environmental situations. If the climate is in particular warm or dry, many springs will quit flowing till conditions enhance.

- Rain Water

Rainfall is one capacity supply of off-grid water. If you live in a wet surroundings, amassing water is every loose and simple. Even higher, rainwater is one of the cleanest simply available assets.

Water may be channeled out of your roof to a garage device using a number one rain accumulating device. It's moreover honest to determine how a notable deal you may seize in a one year. For each inch of rainfall, each square foot of roof region captures 623 gallons of water. Determine the rectangular pix of your roof and investigate nearby rainfall estimates. Even a tiny domestic with only hundred rectangular ft of roof surface might provide about a hundred twenty five gallons of freshwater consistent with inch of rainfall.

Rivers, Streams, and Ponds in their Natural Condition

People had been harnessing obviously flowing water for a long term. Many might possibly-be off-grid population query why they cannot clearly use water from their belongings's herbal springs, streams, ponds, and rivers.

Unfortunately, there are fantastically sturdy factors closer to counting on this water supply. To begin with, it's miles unlawful in maximum of the US and the relaxation of the planet. Western states depend on Appropriative Water Rights to installation who has access to sincerely to be had water. Without stepping into prison jargon, most western assets owners do no longer very own the rights to the water on their property.

You can be fined if you cast off water from a river or one-of-a-kind evidently occurring supply. It's superb that you'd be caught or fined for taking flight a few hundred gallons in step with twelve months. But I do now not recommend violating the regulation to accumulate water.

Buy and Store Water

While no longer exactly in keeping with the concept of off-grid existence, it is practicable to shop for water and transfer it once more to your own home. The most common technique for reaching that is to characteristic a water tank inner or tow behind your automobile.

The professionals are that you only get what you need and might gain greater on every occasion you require it. The drawbacks are self-glaring. Buying water and riding it to your house puts you vulnerable to problems with the grid. It also can be inconvenient, especially if you do not already journey into metropolis for unique requirements on a normal basis.

Bulk water isn't available anywhere, but most RV parks and precise regions with severa web page traffic may additionally have some alternatives.

Running Water Off the Grid

There are crucial technologies that deliver strolling water on the equal time as off-grid. The first opportunity, gravity-fed storage, has been deployed for millennia and employs gravity to transport water through your pipes.

Water will actually go through your pipes as long as your water tank is better than your home. Municipal water towers hire the equal generation to deliver water stress to grid-associated houses.

The advantages of this technique are glaring, but there are a few boundaries. First, you need to deliver the water to that top. This can show up actually if your property has a rain amassing gadget or a well above it. Otherwise, you can have to manually pump water right right into a garage tank. A motorized pump is a few different possibility for producing flowing water. Solar electric powered nicely pumps can also with out troubles deliver pressurized water to an off-grid family.

Pumps with any gallon steady with minute go together with the drift rate are available. They produce strong water pressure however need a regular pull of electricity.

The pumps themselves do not provide steady water stress. A pressurized water tank is maximum usually hired. They make benefit of compressed air garage this is shaped due to the fact the tank fills. When you devour water and the pressure falls, the well pump kicks in and re-pressurizes the tool.

Water Capture and Use Off The Grid

There are numerous techniques for catching and storing water on your off-grid living. These differ relying at the source of your water.

Manual Well Pumps

Manual well pumps are one of the to begin with-grid water systems. If you have got ever watched an antique Western movie, you could consider the repetitious sounds a metal properly pump created at the same time as pushing water up from loads of toes deep.

These are brilliant times of previous era that's despite the fact that applicable in recent times. Manual well pumps are both less expensive and powerful in pulling water from shallow wells. However, the negatives considerably outnumber the rewards. The depth to which guide nicely pumps may additionally draw water is severely constrained. This is typically seventy five m/250 toes for most people. Water can't be pulled with definitely human strength past that restriction.

They moreover do no longer create pressurized water within the same manner that an electric powered pump does. You should first drain the water proper right into a gravity-fed gadget or every different cistern, then upload an electric powered pump. This makes having on foot water a notable deal more difficult. They can be a totally practical possibility in case you preference to stay a lower once more-to-nature way of lifestyles off-grid. Electric pumps, but, are a most suitable possibility for almost all of humans.

Solar and electric powered powered properly pumps

The maximum contemporary electric powered powered nicely pumps may additionally moreover produce massive water glide from even the personal wells. They have modest energy intake and are robust sufficient to offer each regular water stress or a gravity-fed cistern device.

Choosing the appropriate well pump to your dreams comes down to three important problems:

• The duration of your nicely shaft.

• Water float rate (measured in gallons consistent with minute/GPM).

• The wanted energy.

The most important prerequisite for a properly pump is that it match into your properly shaft. It makes no difference how super a pump is if it's miles efficaciously ineffectual for you. The next step is to evaluate how hundreds capability you want. Well pumps can offer the proper go with the flow price.

This controls what number of gallons in keeping with minute your properly pump can deal with. The very last problem to take into account is the energy drain. Evaluate how a good deal power a well pump requires to determine whether or not or now not your gift device can address it. Every 3 hundred and sixty five days, off-grid solar grows much less luxurious and higher. Increasing the functionality of your sun device to strength a properly ought to now not be too high-priced.

Cisterns

It may be required to hold vast portions of water depending at the supply of your water deliver. The maximum possibly resources of cisterns are rainfall and spring water. Cisterns have been initially a form of enclosed underground water garage. They collected rainwater and stored it for use all through dry seasons. Cisterns presently are seeking advice from any form of water garage tank, above or underneath floor. Large plastic tanks are the most commonplace cisterns used for off-grid living, but you can furthermore buy ones composed of metal, cement, or perhaps stone.

For maximum off-grid programs, I need polyethylene garage tanks. They are plenty less expensive, extra long lasting, and withstand microbial increase better than natural substances. They're additionally extensively lighter and much much less hard to move at the same time as empty.

You ought to have an extensive garage plan in location if you installation a rain catchment system. A cistern makes it honest to keep rainwater over time. If you vicinity your cistern nicely, gravity can also moreover even useful useful resource in providing water strain.

Chapter 10: Rainwater Collecting Systems

Rain catchment devices absorb rainwater because it falls passively. Most human beings lease their roof as the most collecting region, funneling water from gutters and drain pipes into plastic rainwater barrels. A rain collecting device is the cheapest and most effective off-grid water machine to assemble, however it has large downsides. Rainwater gathering is great viable on select out types of roofs.

Metal roofs are the nicest, on the equal time as tile and slate are possibility possibilities. Never swallow water accrued from an asphalt roof. It is right for watering your lawn, but it carries too many functionality pollution from the roof fabric to drink.

Once you've caught the water, you want to discover how to make use of it. Some rainwater catchment systems gather the water in immoderate tanks. These are excellent for a gravity-fed machine. It furthermore makes it smooth to region a filtration tool among the water garage and your own home.

Off Grid Water Filtration & Treatment

Once you've acquired a robust supply of water, you need to clean out or deal with it. Some sources are cleaner than others, however I commonly consider it's terrific to be secure than sorry even as health and well being is worried.

The best answers for purifying water off grid are inline and gravity-fed water filtration gadgets. Inline filters hyperlink into your pipes and automatically filter all water getting into your house.

They're the maximum herbal water filters to apply but need greater extensive plumbing facts and flowing water to function. The maximum inside your approach and most clean water filters to location up are gravity filters. They function by the usage of pouring water into an aperture on the pinnacle and allowing it adventure its manner down thru clean out additives.

Gravity-fed filters, just like the Big Berkey water clean out depicted above or the Alexapure water easy out, are low in value, clean to keep, and need zero plumbing to feature. They're excellent if you need a probable basic approach to purifying off-grid water with out managing some of more difficult paintings.

The exemption to the filtering regulation is water meant for irrigation and out of doors usage. There's no point to clear out water which you're truly going to throw immediately onto your plants in the long run.

How to Maintain Off Grid Systems in Winter

Preparation for the wintry weather months is critical to assure you're capable of amplify the life cycle of your off-grid power device; especially if you dwell in cold climes or in a region prone to snow, even in case you stay in a warmer, dryer place, now may be a remarkable possibility to look at the safety everyday and the condition of your machine.

Think Carefully About Solar Panel Positioning

Some large systems include an adjustable rack mount for sun panels, so if you have the kind of, it's a first rate concept to area it at an attitude that could acquire the most of the wintry weather moderate. The suitable angle may moreover additionally make a main impact on the subject of the amount of energy that is captured with the useful resource of using the tool. This is specially essential at the shorter or cloudier days at the same time as sunlight hours is in particular restrained.

The nice panel function is commonly the range of your location, plus 15 tiers or so. This results inside the most appropriate attitude to take gain of the sun.

Keep Clear as Much as Possible

Remembering to dispose of snow, leaves and additional moisture is critical inside the route of wintry climate. Keeping a brush or a brush with an extended cope with nearby ensures you may smooth up snow, dirt, and water routinely.

This is particularly essential at some point of snowy or sub-0 cold intervals as it will take extensively longer in your panels to acquire any sun radiation if the panel is blanketed in snow or ice. Clearing the panels periodically so that you may additionally moreover take gain in case you're out and about and the clouds abruptly deliver manner to a chunk of brightness.

Chapter 11: Generator Maintenance

Now is also the right time to don't forget about generator protection as properly. Aside from the necessities, together with oil belts, coolant, air filters, and spark plugs, it's crucial to go to your proprietor manual to confirm you're preserving any version-particular additives.

It's an notable idea to assess your beginning battery too; if your generator hasn't ran often due to the fact the previous wintry weather, it may need to be replaced or recharged earlier than it is carried out.

Off-Grid Batteries

It is feasible to maintain your batteries in a pretty bloodless environment, but there are few things you want to preserve in mind finally of winter, which includes:

- The strength storage functionality of your batteries at freezing temperatures is reduced momentarily. Instruments in conjunction with battery video display gadgets may be used to decide a more correct rate situation.

• Battery temperature sensors on your rate controller and your inverter need to also be used to make sure that your batteries are at their maximum useful charging positions.

• A battery at entire rate, operated on a ordinary foundation, will no longer freeze till the temps goes underneath -fifty six° Whereas batteries in more or less a 50 percent degree of rate, may moreover freeze in temperatures of round -23°C.

• Don't permit your battery charge to go too low. The sulfuric acid within the batteries at the same time as handiest used now and again might probable stratify. This results in smaller liquid layers at the pinnacle of the battery and heavier layers of sulfuric acid accumulating inside the course of the lowest. When this happens, it's viable that the thinner layer might also freeze and make bigger fractures in the shell of the battery.

Ongoing Maintenance

Extended Leave

If your energy gadget is left unattended for prolonged intervals of time, in conjunction with vacation houses for instance, you want to make provisions to assure that your device remains in terrific situation until your return.

Flooded lead-acid batteries live great while they are utilized on a regular foundation, consequently depending to your set up and machine, there are some matters you may do:

If you operate an automated generator begin collectively at the side of your inverter and also you've invested in a extraordinary generator, there's no purpose why you can't hold the inverter on so there's an without delay accessible price within the case of inclement weather or solar panel blockage. If you don't have an automatic generator begin, make certain superb the inverter is switched off, at the facet of all of the Direct Current loads.

Instead, leave the rate controller strolling, so as a minimum there can be some go with the flow rate to the batteries to preserve them crammed up.

Fine-Tuning & Understanding the Weather in Your Area

We all realize that the sun has a bent to be a rare presence within the course of wintry weather, so it's vital which you take gain of the incredible days once they do get up. Any device proprietor will want to discover how their system responds to common charging and battery equalizing. This is why it's important to maintain in mind boosting absorption times and the equalize settings on your charge controller during the less warm months of the 12 months.

It can also be an tremendous concept to maintain a notice of the seasonal settings which you find out paintings tremendous in your vicinity. This manner, you don't need to spend time messing together along with your settings whenever the seasons trade. Search mode at the inverter need to be engaged year spherical, however this can grow to be greater important in some unspecified time within the future of these less heat months.

When search mode is on, electricity intake on the inverter shifts to no-load operation and is reduce with the resource of roughly 70 percentage.

In this feature, the multi is have end up off in the occasion of no-load or a totally low load, and activates every few seconds for a short period. Should the output cutting-edge-day benefit a described degree, the inverter will shut down all another time. The more numerous hundred watt-hours every day can also make a massive effect.

Increasing Solar Panel Coverage

There's no answer to how many sun panels you have to have, however usually speaking, the extra you have were given, the greater power you may capture. Whether you have to raise the amount you've got honestly is based totally totally on budget and the seasonal situations that impact your region. The remaining purpose is to maximise the herbal resource of the solar so you also can lessen down to your dependency on generator and gas use.

Alternatively, as many who stay off-grid will let you know, it's sincerely genuinely a question of altering your behavior particularly during wintry climate — that is extra critical thinking about that you will be at domestic extra due to the pandemic.

For example, strolling the bathing device typically an afternoon is definitely fantastic while you're having a pleasing sunny day. But, if you're confronted with a horrible, moist day, then you definately simply need to don't forget only cleansing the requirements. Of route, you'll nevertheless have your batteries and generator to hotel to in an emergency, however once more, you're searching for to reduce your dependence on the ones. In the prevent, it's the clean way of life adjustments that makes all the difference, which includes converting your moderate bulbs with LED's or eco-bulbs.

Chapter 12: What Is Living Off The Grid?

Living off the grid has gained a massive following in modern-day years way to movie star endorsements and the growing trouble for the surroundings similarly to at least one's protection. So, it received't be hyperbolic to say that nearly all and sundry has heard of it from one deliver or some different. Yet, before shifting immediately to the basics of living off the grid, it is critical to understand what this concept entails and what it does no longer.

Different people define dwelling off-grid in every other manner. For example, a teenager or a younger man or woman may additionally additionally outline dwelling off grid as dwelling without social media or similar stuff. A spy or a crook can also additionally define it as being untraceable, unrecognizable, and lots of others. A sportsman may define it as dwelling on the 'fringe of the arena.' Although a majority of those definitions are perfectly valid, they may be no longer applicable to the subject of this e-book.

Living off grid approach residing a life of self-sufficiency by using way of the usage of making use of the minimum resources to be had – your reliability on water, strength and waste control need to be the naked minimum! A family can emerge as clearly off-grid at the equal time as it is self-sustained and produces its very very own strength and water at the same time as eliminating its waste successfully.

Most people apprehend that we stay on the electrical grid. Basically, in case your city factors strength to your own home, you and your property are considered to be at the grid. This energy is often maintained and furnished by using an electric corporation. Everything that influences the electric enterprise will have an impact to your electricity supply as properly. For example, if a nice malfunction takes region at the electrical agency, you may go through a strength outage. Thus, you want to rely upon the enterprise enterprise. This is known as residing 'at the grid.'

Living off-grid is the opposite of the above scenario. Living off-grid inside the above situation is probably forgoing strength truely, i.E., living without strength or generating your very own power with a self-sustained supply. This will can help you be self-reliant.

People frequently hold in mind that dwelling off grid best incorporates electricity. However, as said in advance in the definition, it moreover calls for a self-sustained method of waste disposal and herbal water. A circle of relatives with the ones 3 facilities may be called a family this is really off-grid. Such a own family also can use an outhouse or separate septic tank for waste disposal and may accumulate potable water from a properly or a few different natural water supply.

Along with the above three developments, humans frequently encompass self-sustained food to be an vital part of residing off the grid.

If this life-style peaks your interest and sounds amusing you then definately definately are within the proper location. This ebook will educate smooth techniques and hints to help you live off the grid effects. Living off the grid may additionally seem quite daunting at the start and it's far in reality now not an easy undertaking. It takes a number of willpower to break loose from the grid and stay that way. However, if you be successful, you may be able to lead a happy and content cloth lifestyle.

People regularly struggle to live off-grid as it is a complex approach. However, you can begin living off-grid grade by grade. For example, you may no longer have a self-sustained electric powered supply; you may continually have a nicely for water supply.

Generally, folks that live in suburbs or small towns can stay off-grid effectively. However, it will become as a substitute hard to perform that in an metropolis or metropolitan scenario. Although difficult, it isn't not possible to perform that. It is feasible to stay off-grid inner a 365 days if you may do a right research and hire the triumphing assets to be had.

It is not any wonder that the sort of families living off the grid is increasing every day. For instance, as consistent with a file posted in 2006, near a hundred 80,000 households lived off the grid in 2006.

The huge variety has continued to rise considerably at a few level inside the numerous years. It is now expected that approximately 1 / four of 1,000,000 households live off the grid within the United States. The massive variety rises to a whopping 1.7 billion global.

This is partly because of the dearth of sources in underdeveloped countries. Yet it is stable to expect that the variety of voluntary off-gridders is high as properly.

Chapter 13: Pros And Cons Of Living Off The Grid

In the very last financial ruin, we observed the fundamentals of dwelling off the grid and what it involves. In this monetary damage permit's have a have a look at some of the professionals and cons.

Living off the grid may additionally moreover sound appealing and daunting on the identical time. It may additionally invoke photographs of tranquility, peace and solitude and it may moreover invoke pix of freezing winters, loss of sanitation, and plenty of others. But those images are hyperbolic. Living off the grid does not 'have' to mean dwelling somewhere faraway from civilization like a caveman. If you still want convincing, here is a short evaluation of the experts and cons of residing off the grid.

Pros of Living off the Grid

Cheap Recurring Rates

Living off the grid is reasonably-priced because you are basically producing nearly everything you want in a sustainable way. Despite the steep charges initially, a renewable supply of power can reduce down your electricity invoice extensively. Although the quantity you keep will variety in line with your location and nation, it is predicted that common economic financial savings from sun panels are about $eighty four. An common solar panel has a lifespan of approximately a long time, so you will emerge as saving spherical $20,000 with solar panel by myself. Combine it with different sustainable belongings and you may see a huge boom to your financial savings.

You also can advantage take gain of solar panels and distinct belongings of sustainable energy via selling energy-to-strength groups. Many states require companies to deliver a certain amount of renewable electricity for performance certificates. These agencies frequently buy such energy from small off-gridders. Although a beneficial approach, now not many off-grid households propose it - in particular for beginners. First, it's miles hard to offer excessive quantities of energy, in particular for novices. Secondly, this method locations you at the grid in a way. Thus, it is completely your preference whether or not or no longer you need to move in advance with the approach or no longer.

Along with strength payments you could also save on water payments via finding or growing a sustainable supply of clean water. This can consist of wells, clean water property which include rivers, lakes or perhaps groundwater reserves.

Flexibility

Another big gain of dwelling off the grid is the strength that it affords. As an off-grid circle of relatives does not need to depend on public resources, it may be located nearly everywhere. For instance, in case you opt for solitude, cute nature and need to avoid the monotonous and irritating town existence then you may flow into to a village and stay surely - way to off-grid residing. Producing your personal strength gives you the freedom of living wherever you need.

If you pick a ways flung locations, it is able to be pretty tough to attach your private home to the grid. In such times, it is quality to stay off the grid. It will will let you stay independently and you could now not ought to pay extra carrier costs truly to connect your own home to the grid. These savings can then be invested in specific, better and important investments.

Environment

Although there are various naysayers, it is not possible to disclaim that our environment is changing unexpectedly. Global warming is an unfortunate but actual phenomenon that cannot be disregarded.

Climate alternate will alter the way we live over the subsequent few a long time. It is, consequently, the need of the time to exchange and start the use of renewable assets of power and start residing sustainably. Living off grid combines every this stuff and is, therefore, one of the high-quality approaches to live.

There are many environmental advantages of dwelling off the grid out of which decreased carbon emission is the maximum giant one. Living off the grid using renewable assets of power such as wind power and sun energy can reduce your carbon footprint appreciably.

Let us now have a have a have a look at some cons of dwelling off the grid.

Cons of Living off the Grid

Logistics

One of the not unusual lawsuits you get to pay attention about living off the grid is the logistics. Renewable power, despite the fact that cheap, isn't always easy to set up. It goals a huge earlier economic funding. For instance, a smooth 5kW sun panel may cost a few factor among $25000 and $35000. Similarly, a 10kW wind turbine may cost a bit a touch round $45000 to $65000. Although sure, you'll advantage returned all the fees and greater with time, the preliminary charge may throw people off the idea of living off the grid.

Another issue about renewable energy is that it's miles more active at sure locations. For example, solar power is straightforward to apply and acquire in sunny places whereas it falters at locations which can be cloudy within the course of the twelve months. Similarly, wind electricity is feasible most effective if you have a massive assets.

Some states provide reasonably-priced on grid electricity, so in case your fundamental reason for going off the grid is cash, it is better to stay at the grid rather.

Hassle

Living off the grid isn't always an clean method. It is a tough preference as well and in case you do it with out adequate planning or studies, you may truely be stricken by approach of terrible repercussions. Making your very very own strength requires some of planning and studies. You need to plot the initial expenses, locations, products and device with the help of right guidebooks and/or specialists.

After fame quo, renewable power systems often require everyday renovation. Solar panels and structures are regularly self-cleaning if the region gets enough precipitation. However, in case you stay in an arid place, it is encouraged to smooth them frequently. You moreover need to run an annual check to make certain that your panels are in reality performing at their complete capability.

In the case of wind energy structures, you need to replace blades and bearing after 10-15 years. You moreover want to test the wires and unique such matters frequently to hold overall performance.

Limited Nature

According to numerous surveys, the residents of the united states use more electricity than maximum human beings the world over. Although energy usage is subjective to various factors which includes the dimensions of your family, your utilization behavior, the variety of gadgets and the sort (kind) you have got. It is frequently visible that renewable electricity systems may not fulfill all your power needs. Users and families with greater power wishes may additionally want to rely upon the grid. People who do not stay in sunny or windy areas may want to depend on the grid as nicely.

If you continue to need to live off the grid then you can ought to adapt and make modifications for your life therefore. You will need to discover ways to conserve strength.

This may also include downsizing electronics and finding some different manner to chill the residence in summer season. All the ones factors can show pretty difficult for people who are privy to a positive popular of residing.

It is right that dwelling off the grid takes time, funding and willpower.

However, if in comparison to the professionals of residing on the grid, they are a lot greater huge than the cons.

If you are geared up to take a piece of greater strive, living off the grid will genuinely display well worth.

How Do You Like The Book So Far?

CLICK HERE TO LEAVE FEEDBACK ON AMAZON

If you're not certain, truly leave a compare later...

Chapter 14: Moving Out Of The City

Moving out is constantly a tough technique fiscally, logistically and emotionally. You need to maintain in mind plenty of things earlier than transferring out to a trendy location. For instance, when you have usually lived in the suburbs, or in a small village, shifting to a metropolis like Los Angeles can also throw you off your stability and manner of lifestyles absolutely. You can also enjoy stressed, befuddled and overwhelmed. Similarly, if you skip out from a big city to a small city or a village, it could overwhelm you. Living off the grid frequently requires moving out. However, now not like 'normal' moving out, you regularly want to move out to a far flung location, with out the centers and facilities of a metropolis or city places. Thus, it calls for sufficient making plans and research.

How to Move Out:

As said in advance, moving out to a far off region, mainly in case you are acquainted with an urban existence may additionally moreover show to be quite daunting and complicated. People residing in towns are frequently used to a pleasing preferred of living this is tough or nearly now not feasible to duplicate an off-grid state of affairs, at least for the duration of the initial tiers. Therefore, the number one trouble that a person wishes to do earlier than moving out is to put together himself for the emotional and physical turmoil. You want to conform and adjust regular together along with your scenario and events otherwise you can no longer be able to stay to tell the story.

One of the quality matters to put together your self mentally and emotionally is with the useful resource of reading memoirs and searching interviews of people who have been dwelling off-grid. These include humans who have been residing off the grid for years further to who have clearly made the exchange. This will help you to recognize the issues and predicaments that human beings face. Such people might also offer you recommendations as a way to make your skip smoother.

Choosing Location:

Choosing a place to stay off the grid may be a hard undertaking for some. The following is a list of worries which you ought to maintain in mind earlier than choosing a area.

It is crucial to select out a land so that it will be appropriate for all your goals. For example, in case you plan to cultivate your own food, attempt to find out a big piece of land this is fertile as well. It is without a doubt vital to apprehend the soil composition of any land that you plan to buy. Similar to land and land homes, it is also crucial to check out the water resources, if any. For instance, in sure states, you do not very very own rights to the water, although it is on your house.

Another issue which you want to consider in advance than choosing a region is whether it gets sufficient daylight and wind to your renewable power systems.

Perks

Certain lands encompass geographical competencies that would display to be assets for you. These embody:

●Natural Gas Wells - Certain non-public residences in positive states of the us very personal private natural gasoline wells. These wells can't most effective be used for heating and gas talents, however you can additionally hire it to gasoline businesses for added earnings.

●Artesian Aquifer - In an artesian aquifer, the water is restrained in layers of rocks therefore staying under strain. This permits the water to waft upward with out pumps.

Housing

The subsequent element to tackle after locating a appropriate location is housing. You need some type of dwelling to stay in. Off-grid livers use quite some brief, eternal and semi-eternal dwellings. Nowadays many recycled alternatives have come to be well-known as nicely.

Two of the most not unusual brief shelters encompass trailers/ RVs and Tents. You can use the ones to stay till your eternal residing is complete.

Of the two options mentioned above, tents are quite cheap. However, they do now not offer sufficient assist and offerings. An RV or trailer can not simplest offer you with all the facilities of a normal house, however it could additionally offer you with the safety and safety in competition to weather and different factors. Although trailers are costly, you may discover cheap 2d-hand trailers on-line. Make positive to test them cautiously earlier than looking for.

Permanent Shelter

You have to customize and adapt your eternal house in line with your location. For example, in case you live in a cold region, customize your property simply so it receives enough daylight at some stage inside the day. This will assist you keep it warmth obviously without the want to spend on searching out offerings to hold the house heat.

Many off-gridders choose out to gather their non-public shelters. Unless you're cushty with device and building substances and characteristic hundreds of free time, please do not attempt to try this.

Chapter 15: Power

The principal idea of dwelling off the grid is self-sustenance; which means that despite the fact that the area is ready to quit, you and your circle of relatives will stay constant and solid. Having your personal energy supply is the first step of self-sustenance. For instance, if there can be a weeklong energy outage inside the course of the metropolis because of a hurricane, you can but have power way on your renewable electricity system. There are severa renewable or wonderful kinds of sustainable strength systems that will let you stay off the grid. Let us have a have a take a look at them one by one.

Geothermal Energy

Geo manner earth and thermal technique warmness, so geothermal electricity method the warm temperature this is acquired from the earth. The temperature rises as you bypass deep within the earth. Geothermal pumps use this principle and pump electricity for heating purposes. Geothermal energy is regularly used for critical heating. These pumps require a good deal less power than ordinary pumps however can warmness the house pretty successfully.

Geothermal strength additionally may be used to warmness water.

Many experiments had been finished at the way to use geothermal energy to generate electricity. Geothermal electricity grow to be first generated in Larderello, Italy in the yr 1904. Today, the USA produces spherical 2,seven hundred megawatts of energy the use of this deliver.

Solar Power

Solar electricity, as the decision indicates is the energy derived from the solar. There are kinds of sun power, passive and energetic. In passive solar strength, no specific device is used to harness the energy. For example, houses get hold of the daylight through the home windows. Another instance of passive sun power is heating water in a swimming pool the usage of the sunrays. You have to constantly try to harness as a good buy passive sun strength viable whilst constructing a residence. This will allow you to lessen bills appreciably.

In energetic sun strength, you need to use specific mechanical devices to apply, preserve, accumulate and distribute solar energy. Generally, solar panels are used to save electricity. These panels convert sun power into power the usage of an inverter. The inverter converts sun power into AC current-day. This cutting-edge can then be used each right now or stored in a battery array for future use.

A sun electric powered array includes the subsequent 5 crucial additives:

Solar panels

These are also known as PV or photovoltaic panels.

Mounting Rack

These are the steel manual structures that maintain the complete device. These are prepared in this kind of manner that the panels face the solar all the time and get maintain of sufficient mild and heat.

Charge Controller:

These control strength among solar powers and the batteries.

Battery Bank:

These are a group of batteries that capture and maintain sun electricity within the form of power.

Inverter:

These convert sun energy into electric powered powered powered AC modern-day for immediate or future use.

Before choosing a sun energy device for your home, you need to determine your requirements and strength consumption.

Wind Power

Wind electricity can prove to be an asset for folks that live in windy regions. Wind strength may be used as a complement to solar electricity, or in regions with ordinary wind, it may even turn out to be the primary deliver of energy.

There are masses of wind strength systems and it is, consequently, essential to recognize your necessities and strength consumption earlier than buying one. Nowadays, hybrid solar cum wind systems are to be had too. These comprise the solar panel alongside facet wind turbines. The combination of those can provide sufficient strength for your own family.

Small wind structures are smooth to installation and acquire. They are regularly rate effective as properly. Generally, such systems encompass a wind turbine together with a battery economic group and an inverter. Like solar energy tool, the inverter converts wind strength into power and the battery financial organization stores it for future use.

For first-class outcomes, you want to area the wind turbine as a minimum a hundred toes immoderate. The winds at this peak are frequently faster and much tons much less turbulent than ordinary winds. The wind blows through the generators and moves them. This rotation effects within the manufacturing of electricity.

Although wind strength was handiest utilized in commercial initiatives earlier than, these days smaller mills were developed that may be used to energy your own home. They take exceptionally a lot less region than regular mills and wonderful models can seize wind from all guidelines.

Hydro Power

Hydro Electricity is one of the most used renewable assets of energy all through the arena. Although huge hydroelectric vegetation are used by electric powered corporations to provide energy all over, you may also use micro-hydro turbines for non-public use.

Hydropower is a long way more powerful than solar or wind power due to the fact it is ordinary and non-save you not much like the opportunity two. In principal duties, dams are used to run hydroelectric turbines. However, in home tasks; you could want a pipe to divert a go with the flow of water inside the direction of your generator. This circulate ought to commonly come from an inexhaustible source of water.

Like specific energy structures, you want to first study your necessities and energy consumptions earlier than searching for a hydroelectric electricity device. You will also need to determine the go along with the go with the flow of water. Unless you've got a vast go with the drift, you might not be capable of produce sufficient electricity to run a everyday own family.

These are some of the primary electric electricity systems that may placed you off the grid. Another vital difficulty about those power systems is that they may be often quite steeply-priced to put in and launch the setup. They require some of time, cash and staying power to install. However, they'll be sincerely clearly worth the trouble as they lessen your bills to nearly zero.

www.ingramcontent.com/pod-product-compliance
Lightning Source LLC
LaVergne TN
LVHW011731280125
802401LV00009B/495